QUR'AN VERSES WHICH STOPPED A JUDEO- CHRISTIAN CONVERTING TO ISLAM

آيات قرآنية حالت دون تحول شخص من ثقافة مسيحية يهودية إلى الإسلام

CONSTANTINE BAR JOB
قسطنطين بن أيوب

LitPrime Solutions
21250 Hawthorne Blvd
Suite 500, Torrance, CA 90503
www.litprime.com
Phone: 1 (209) 788-3500

© 2021 Constantine Bar Job. All rights reserved.

No part of this book may be reproduced, stored in a retrieval system, or transmitted by any means without the written permission of the author.

Published by LitPrime Solutions   03/03/2021

ISBN: 978-1-953397-56-0(sc)
ISBN: 978-1-953397-57-7(hc)
ISBN: 978-1-953397-58-4(e)

Library of Congress Control Number: 2020924747

Any people depicted in stock imagery provided by iStock are models, and such images are being used for illustrative purposes only.

Certain stock imagery © iStock.

Because of the dynamic nature of the Internet, any web addresses or links contained in this book may have changed since publication and may no longer be valid. The views expressed in this work are solely those of the author and do not necessarily reflect the views of the publisher, and the publisher hereby disclaims any responsibility for them.

QUR'AN VERSES WHICH STOPPED A JUDEO- CHRISTIAN CONVERTING TO ISLAM

CONSTANTINE BAR JOB

When a Christian friend of mine knew that I wanted to convert to Islam he warned me that the first thing I have to do is to have the foreskin of my penis cut off & if for one reason or another I apostate then I have to be ready to have my head cut off. I told him that I am already circumcised & I was very confident that I will never apostate.

Fortunately, the information in this book spared me my head & I hope it will spare the heads of many

INTRODUCTION

I (the author) was born & grew up in a Judeo-Christian environment. My father is a strict Jew from Russia and my mother is a committed Christian from Bulgaria. They had civil wedding because my father would not get married in a Church & my mother refused to get married in a Synagogue, yet their civil wedding was blessed by a Rabbi & a Priest.

The love my parents have for each other is noticeable in everything they do & I always wished if I ever get married to have an ideal family life like theirs.I am their only son. I asked my mother why they did not have more children. She told me there was difficulty in conception.

My father wants me to be a Jew & my mother wants me to be Christian. Both of them are doing their best to make me follow their religious beliefs. I go with my father regularly to the Synagogue & I go with my mother to Church whenever possible. She keeps telling me that Christ fulfilled all the prophecies of the Old Testament and He is the Messiah the Jews are still vainly waiting for.

When I was young my father wanted me to be circumcised but my mother did not agree because in her mind that would confirm that I am a Jew. However, she eventually agreed to my circumcision on the basis that I would be baptised as well & it would be up to me to decide whether to be a Jew or a Christian when I grow up. It was a strange agreement between them. Every time I go to the Synagogue I wear the skullcap (kippah) & my father is very proud of me, and when I go to Church I always join my mother

& have the Holy Communion which pleases her immensely. In fact I am torn between both religions. It is difficult for me to decide which one to chose for good, though my inclination is slightly more towards Christianity.

At university I became very friendly with a guy (a fellow student) from India. We spent most of the time together. What struck me about him is the number of times he prays, to an extent that we would be walking together & then he would say it is time to pray. He would take a handkerchief out of his pocket, spread it on the ground in a corner, kneel & start praying. Initially it looked weird to me to see someone praying so frequently. I asked him why he prays so often. He told me it is essential to do that in Islam. Of course I had to respect that & it did not affect our relationship in any way. He was an excellent guy & a very good friend.

On a few occasions we were walking by a Mosque & he excused himself to go in & pray while I waited outside. One time he told me to wait for him inside the Mosque standing or squatting at the back, while he prayed, hesitantly I did. I was amazed by the way they stand in lines, kneel together & stand up together in silence while the leader recites verses from the Qur'an. The whole atmosphere looked very pious and serene. I happened to attend the Mosque a number of times after that with my good friend. Every time I came out of the Mosque with the same feeling of peace, content & piety.

One day my friend asked me about my thoughts & my opinion of what I saw & experienced. I told him that I was very impressed indeed, A year went by & I was going to a Mosque on a Friday, a Synagogue on a Saturday & a Church on a Sunday.

My parents knew that my best friend is a Moslem & that I have been with him occasionally to a Mosque. They never objected.

One day my good friend asked me if I would ever consider converting to Islam. I told him that I have been thinking about it but I need to know more. So he gave me an English translation of the Qur'an to enlighten me. I took the book home with me, it was dinner time. As I sat at the table with the book by my side my father asked me what that book is about. I told him it was the Qur'an and that I will be converting to Islam. As soon as I said that I felt the atmosphere got electrified. The usual jolly talk we exchanged turned into complete silence. I could feel they were not sure what to do or say. All of us were forcing food down our throats in order to kill time so that there would be no chance to talk. The situation was very tense. Their facial expressions were very unnerving. I never experienced anything like it at home before. In the end I could not tolerate the situation any longer, I excused myself to go to my room as I had lots of homework to do.

I went & laid on my bed thinking what on earth have I done. About an hour later my father knocked on my door & came in. I could tell he was most probably crying because his eyes were red like I have never seen before & he was continuously sniffing as if to clear the tears from his nose. He sat at the foot of my bed facing me & looking straight at me. He said "Son, I want to ask you a big favour & I want you to promise that you will do it ". I said "Dad, I will do anything you ask me as I have always done but please do not ask me not to convert to Islam ".He replied "You can convert with our blessing providing you actually do our favour and what we request from you ". I asked "And what is that you want me to do ". He said "promise to convert only after you have studied Islam & what it is all about. If by then you still want to convert then go ahead, its your life & you would have taken that decision after a thorough educated assessment of Islam." I told him "Dad, that is why I brought this Qur'an with me." He said "No, that is not enough. There are two pillars of Islam. They are inseparable from each other.One is the Qur'an which states what Islam is all about & the other is called Al-Hadeeth which explains the deeds and sayings of their prophet Mohammad. Both must be studied in Arabic, not in English, because the English translation will never convey the same meaning which is stated in the Qur'an or Al-Hadeeth." I said to him "but Dad you know I don't read Arabic." He replied "Well, that is your mission then before conversion, & if you get convinced after all of these studies that you must convert to Islam we will respect your decision, who knows may be I and your Mum will follow in your steps knowing that our intelligent son has converted after studying Islam thoroughly. Probably we are missing something about Islam that has not been exposed to us before in our lives." I smiled and gave him a solemn promise that is what I will do. He smiled back at me, stood up, came to me, shook my hand & gave me a kiss on my cheek, bid me good night & left my room.

It took me three years studying Arabic & I became good reading & understanding it without making mistakes.Meanwhile my friendship with my good Moslem friend became even stronger & I kept reading the English translation of the Qur'an whenever I could.

The time came when I thought that I should start studying the Qur'an in Arabic & I will follow that by Al-Hadeeth. I started making notes of things which were not acceptable to me or which did not make sense to me.

By the time I finished reading the Qur'an in Arabic I must admit I never had the same sense of meaning when I read the English translation.However, I eventually realised that there are many things in the Qur'an I found difficult to apply in real life, for various reasons. I concluded by then that Islam is definitely not for me. I told my good friend about my decision which he took wholeheartedly & we remained very good friends. On that same day, as I was having dinner with my parents, I told them that after reading and thoroughly studying the Qur'an I have decided not to convert to Islam.I could tell that Mum & Dad were very pleased to hear that, especially my Mum, she started crying with Joy. My father asked me what do I think of Al-Hadeeth. I told him that what I read in the Qur'an was enough to make my final decision. There was no need for me to study Al-Hadeeth

With regards to my future, I am not sure if I will end up a Jew or a Christian. I have to read the Old & the New Testaments thoroughly to make my final way in life.

My father said "Son. we are sure that you made the right decision regarding your conversion., we will have to wait & see whether you will end up a Jew or a Christian. In either case it will be an excellent idea to write your thoughts & experience in a book to enlighten others who are seriously thinking of converting to Islam".After a period of reflection I thought that is what I will do & here it is :

PREFACE

Regarding Organising This Book

It was my intention in the beginning to write this book in English, then I realised that some people might complain that my translation of the verses is not what the verses in the Qur'an mean.

We all know that translating something from one language to another is not very easy.

One cannot translate word for word & a phrase for a phrase, if one is to get across the exact meaning of the original text. Sometimes a whole sentence replaces one word because a similar word does not exist in the other language, also some words might have a meaning which a corresponding word in the other language could mean something else if used in the same context.

With regards to the Qur'an, some verses are very straight forward & the meaning glares you in the eye, other verses are very difficult to understand, even to people who are very well versed in the Arabic language. What is worse is the presence of a few verses even the most learned in Islamic Religion give conflicting opinions as to what theses verses mean. Just to give you an example – Does the sun set in a hot water spring, or does it set in hot black mud, or does it set in hot muddy water, is anybody's guess. In this situation I translated it as hot spring because I found this the most logical & suitable place for the sun to set in (though it is not what I believe). There are a number of similar situations which I intentionally avoided, in order not to fall into the trap of misrepresenting the meaning of what was revealed in the Qur'an.

As one can see, translation can be very difficult and I found that the Qur'an verses are the most difficult of all. I had to dig deep to get the true meaning of the verses. Sometimes it took me hours to translate one verse, so one can feel the amount of work that has gone into this book,

As a consequence of all the above and as I now consider my Arabic language to be good, I have decided to write this book in both English & Arabic. The English translation will be on the left hand side & the Qur'an Verses in Arabic (excluding my foot notes of course) on the right hand side. It is written chapter for chapter (The relevant chapters are numbered exactly in the order they appear in the Qur'an), verse number for verse number (Also as in the Qur'an) & page for page. This will make it very easy for the reader to compare between the English and Arabic sections of the book. The Arabic Qur'an verses are exactly as that of Hafs version of the Qur'an written in modern Arabic. This is because Hafs version is the most in common use.

Therefore, the intention of writing in both languages is for those people who query my translation, yet can read Arabic and are well versed in it. It would be very easy for them to refer straight away to the Arabic section of the book & check the authenticity of the Qur'an verses & the quality of my translation. They will notice that I have conveyed the translated message of the verses in the best way possible without the slightest intention of misinterpretation, deviation or misleading the English reader.

A few verses were too long to translate and their full translation would not have added anything to the content if this book, In these situations I only quoted the phrase/s which I found unacceptable in these verses, and recorded the phrases between inverted commas. So my translation would be for what was quoted between the inverted commas only.

On each page of the main body of the book is written the verses of the Qur'an that I cannot live with or cannot accept for various reasons, with a short footnote of my explanation.

Please note that throughout the book the singular is referred to as plural when God is mentioned, because in the Arabic language the plural signifies might, greatness & the highest seat of authority.

In certain places I have added words between brackets to identify the previous word or explain a previous phrase or sentence. this is to simplify to the reader what the verse of the Qur'an is saying.

There are certain words or phrases in the Holy Qur'an that are very difficult to translate & give the exact meaning, for example :

1 – The word "Superior" "أولياء" which I used in the text on several occasions could also mean controller or leader. It simply refers to people who are superior to you and have the authority to control you.

2 – The phrase "what your right hand owns" "ما ملكت أيمانهم" is mentioned frequently in the Holy Qur'an. It simply means women who one owns as part of the spoils of war or who were bought as part of a merchandise. Their numbers could be anything from one to thousands, They were also a sign of status in the community. The only word I could use to explain this in my translation is "Captives".

3 – Throughout the text I used the word "Plundering ""غنائم"" to describe the situation following acts of raids, invasion, attacks or all out war. These acts consisted of taking land, possessions,

killing men, taking women as captives & taking children to keep them as slaves or to exchange them for weapons/arms …etc.

4 – The Arabic word "Nikaah" "نكاح" appears in the Holy Qur'an on many occasions and in many Suwar (plural for Surat/ Surah). When I checked the Arabic dictionary for the meaning of this word it was & still is "sexual intercourse". I queried this word being used so frequently in the Holy Qura'an with my good friend & other Moslems I met at the Mosque including the Imam (the head of the Mosque). All of them told me that this word means wedding in the Holy Qur'an. Apparently, when people get married in Islam they get what is called a "Nikaah Contract".

My shock came when I read Surat Al-Ahzab -33 Verse 37 regarding God allowing the prophet Muhammad to marry his adopted son's wife. Its Verse mentions very clearly the word "Zawwajnakaha" "زوجناكها" which when I checked its meaning in the Arabic dictionary it means "wed her to you". Then I thought to myself if "Zawaj" means wedding in Arabic then why didn't the Holy Qur'an use this word rather than the rude "Nikaah" throughout the Holy Qur'an. Moreover, if "Nikaah" means wedding, Then why God didn't say to the prophet Muhammad in Surat Al-Ahzab 33 Verse 37 "Nakkahnakaha" نكحناكها in stead of "Zawwajnakaha". The whole thing seems very confusing indeed.

SURAT AL-BAQARAH -2

Verse 22 –He who flattened the earth and structured the heaven for you & brought down water from heaven which resulted in fruits for your sustenance, so don't take any rivals to God. You should know this.

The earth is not flat, it is round

Verse 29-He (God) created everything on earth for you, then settled in heaven and made them seven heavens and He knows everything.

As far as I know there are no seven heavens

Verse 65-And you know those amongst you who violate the Sabbath. We said to them be despised monkeys.

Why would God make monkeys out of human beings.

Verse 106-No verse do we cancel or cause to be forgotten without replacing it with a better or a similar one. Didn't you know that God is capable of everything.

How come God's revelations are not absolutely faultless from the very beginning but can be replaced or improved upon. This means that God also can make mistakes.

Verse 161-Those who were infidels and died as infidels, they have on them the curse of God, the angels and all the people.

Why would God, the angels and all the people curse anyone.

Verse 193 – And fight them so there will be no sedition & religion will be to God. There will b e no enmity if they desist, except against the oppressors.

God spreading the message through force

Verse 216-Fighting is written for you and you hate it, may be you hate something which is good for you and may be you like something and it is bad for you. God knows and you don't know.

Why should fighting be written for anybody?

Verse 223-Your women are your tilth, so come to your tilth whenever you like. Give something from yourselves & fear God, know that you are going to meet Him, with good tidings to the believers.

Why are women looked at as tilth to be tilthed any time.

Verse 225-God does not take it against you if you speak what is not in your heart regarding your faith, but He will for what is really in your hearts, because God is forgiving and merciful.

God is asking his followers to lie and be hypocritical.

Verse 230-If he (the husband) divorces her (his wife), she is not allowed for him until she gets married to another husband, if he (the other husband) divorces her, then there is nothing wrong for both of them (the original couple) to go back together, if they so wish, as long as they keep God's limits, which He declares for people who understand.

I find this too much of a punishment for both parties

SURAT AL-IMRAN-3

Verse 6-He (God) who forms you in the womb as He wishes. There is no God but Him. The dear, the wise.

It does not make sense nowadays with cloning and medical interference

Verse 28-Let not the believers take the infidels as their superiors rather than the believers. Whoever does that, God has nothing to do with him, except if you do it to protect yourself from them. God himself warns you & to him is the aim

Why shouldn't the believers take the infidels as their masters? Sometimes the infidels are much better than the believers. God is asking his followers to be hypocritical towards others

Verse - 54 And they were cunning and God was cunning . God is the best in cunning

It is totally unacceptable to attribute cunningness to God

Verse 106-The day some faces are whitened and others are blackened, but those whose faces were blackened did they disbelieve after believing, then taste the torture of your infidelity.

This sounds like divine racial discrimination against black people

Verse 107-But those whose faces were whitened are in the everlasting grace of God

It seems God favours white people to blacks. This is unbelievable and one of the most racially discriminatory divine statements. What about coloured people who are neither black or white.

Verse 151-We (God) will throw terror in the hearts of those who did not believe, for they believed in others than what we authoritatively provided. Their refuge is fire and the worse place of tyrants.

I cannot believe that God throws terror in the hearts of anyone

Verse 167- Let those hypocrites know, they were told come and fight for the sake of God or pay, they said, if we knew there was fighting we could have joined you, then they were closer to non-belief than to faith. Their mouths say what is not in their hearts and God knows what they conceal

Why God wants people to fight for Him? He can send an army of angels to fight for him in stead.

Verse 195-Their God responded to them, I do not waste the deed of a doer amongst you, be it a male or a female, you are members of each other. Those who emigrated & were forced out of their homes, & were harmed for my sake, & fought & were killed, I will forgive them their sins, & will admit them to gardens with ever flowing rivers underneath, coming from God & He has good rewards.

Why would one fight & get killed to be rewarded by worldly things

SURAT AL-NISA'-4

Verse 3-If you are afraid not to be fair to the orphans, get married to what you like, to two, three or four women, but, if you cannot treat them equally, then(get married to) one, and what you own of captives. This is the least for you not to be unjust.

Why can men have so many wives & captives. It demeans women.

Verse 15-Those of your women who become lustful, get four witnesses to witness against them, and if they do, then keep them (the women) at home until they die or God finds them some other way.

Verse 3 above allows men to do almost whatever they want, but women get penalised whatever they do.

Verse 24-Married women are not allowed to you except those whom you own as captives, and you are allowed other than that what you can get with your money of the not allowed women for pleasure providing you pay them their due with mutual consent. God was all knowing & wise.

What is the difference between this and payment for sex

Qur'an Verses which stopped a Judeo- Christian converting to Islam | 17

Verse 25-Those of you who haven't got the resources to have sexual intercourse with married believers, you can do with young female believers whom you own as captives. God knows of your beliefs, members of each other, so have sexual intercourse with them with their relatives permission and pay them their due with gratitude. They should be chase, not vile, not taking lovers. If they become shameful, their punishment is half that of married women. This is for those amongst you who are afraid of sin, but it is better for you if you are patient. God is merciful & forgiving.

This verse supports the previous verse 24. Promoting sex for money.

Verse 34-Men are dominant over women. God has preferred some to others for what they provide with their money. The good ones (women) are aware of what God has provided in their absence. Those of whom you fear disloyalty, reprimand them, don't sleep (have sexual intercourse) with them and beat them. If they obey, you should not have grudges against them. God is high & great.

I hate to see my father beating my mother, and I would never beat my wife come what may. Moreover, why should God prefer some to others especially if they provide Him with money.

The good ones (women) who are aware of what God has provided in their absence must be the naïve women.

This is probably one of the worse verses I read in the Qur'an. I cannot believe that women can accept this humiliating and demeaning commandment from their God.

Verse 43-O you who believed, don't approach prayer while drunk, unless you know what you are saying.there is no guilt except for those who are on the road, until you wash, or, if you were sick, or travelling, or one of you comes from defecation, or you touch women, or you find no water. Then take soil and rub with it your faces & hands. God is merciful & forgiving.

I find it extremely difficult to equate my mother, my wife whom I touch on a regular basis, my female relatives & acquaintances to excrement. Moreover to clean myself with soil from the ground which contain all kinds of dirt is beyond me.

Verse 74-Let those who seek the second life for this one get killed for the sake of God. Who fights for the sake of God & gets killed or wins, will be given a great reward.

Why are people rewarded for killing or being killed?

Verse 75-Why aren't you fighting for the sake of God & the weakened amongst men, women & children. These people say, our God get us out of this tyrannously populated village, and let one of your followers be our protector & victor.

Here again God is asking people to fight. Aren't there other means of dealing with tyranny? How is it that even ordinary people seek peaceful & friendly coexistence, yet God who is supposed to be the most loving always seeks fighting.

Verse 76-Those who believe fight for the sake of God, & the infidels fight for the sake of calamity. So fight the supporters of the devil. The vindictiveness of the devil is weak.

Yet again we are expected to fight.

Verse 77-Can't you see those who were told stop what you are doing & establish prayer and give to charity. When ordered to fight, some of them seem to fear people as much as they fear God, & even more. They said, God, why have you ordered us to fight now, couldn't you have postponed it a short while. Say the pleasure of the world is little, the eternal is better to the pious & you will not be unjustified at all.

Another verse enticing people to fight.

Verse 82- Don't they consider the Qur'an, had it not been from God they would have found in it many inconsistencies.

Could there be more inconsistencies than that. Many verses ask for peace, forgiveness & good deeds yet others ask for killing, violence & terror.

Verse 84- Then fight for the sake of God & look only after yourself. Entice the believers so that God will curb the might of those who disbelieved. God is much mightier & more baleful.

God is asking people to fight for Him, yet asks his prophet to look only after himself.

Verse 89-They want you to disbelieve like they do. Don't take them as your superiors until they emigrate wherever God sends them. If they turn back, take them & kill them wherever you find them & don't take from them a superior or a backer.

Not trusting anyone else other than your own people, also reference to violence towards others.

Verse 91-You will find others who want to be on your good side and the good side of their people. Every time they went back to discordance, they yielded to it. If they don't leave you or make peace with you & repress their hands, then take them & kill them wherever you find them. We have provided you with authority over them.

Isn't there a more lenient way dealing with things. God is supposed to be against violence by all means.

Verse 144-O you who believed infidels rather than the believers as your superiors, do you surely want God to be against you.

Another example of hatred towards other people ordained by God?!

Verse 176- "The share of the male is twice that of the female"

What is fair about the disparity between the genders? It seems God prefers males to females.

SURAT AL-MA'IDA -5

Verse 6-You who have believed, if you are ready for prayer, wash your faces & your hands to the elbows, and wash your heads & your legs to the ankles, & if you were dirty clean yourselves. If you were sick or travelling, or one of you comes from defecation, or touched women & find no water, use soil to clean your faces & your hands. God does not want to embarrass you but to make you clean & his blessing upon you is complete. so be thankful.

Yet again why equate women to excrement & how come one can clean one's self with soil.

Verse 33-It is the penalty of those who wage war against God and his messenger, and seek trouble in the land, to be killed, or crucified or have their hands and legs cut off from the opposite side, or be exiled from the land. That will be shame for them in this world,& there will be severe punishment for them in the afterlife.

To me this is brutality on an unprecedented scale.

Verse 37-As to a male or a female thief, cut off their hands as a punishment for what they have stolen. This is penalty from God And God is dear & wise.

Imagine having my hand cut off because I stole a piece of bread for my hungry child. Can God be so cruel to punish people in this way? Certainly there is a place for compassion in this world. May be we can come up with a better way dealing with thieves, such as tying their hands in handcuffs to shame them for a period of time.

Verse 51-O you who believed, don't take the Jews and the Christians as your superiors, they are members of each other, & who accepts them, then he is one of them. God does not shield the oppressors.

What is this hatred towards Jews and Christians. I cannot feel that towards my Jewish father and my Christian mother who have never done me any harm & both love me to bits.

Verse 60 – Shall I tell you something worse than this, as decreed by God. Those who incurred the wrath of God & were transformed into apes & pigs (Jews & Christians) & worshipped the devil. They are in a worse position & have strayed the true path.

Why think of Jews as apes & Christians as pigs?!

Verse 101-O you who believed, do not ask about things which seem disturbing to you. God will reveal them to you if you ask about them when the Qur'an is available. God is forgiving & tolerant.

I think it is essential for human beings to ask & enquire about everything to reach the ultimate truth. Why the Qur'an does not want us to ask about things we are not sure of or which seem to be disturbing to us.

SURAT AL-A'RAF -7

Verse 99-Are they secured of the cunning of God. Only the scorned people will not be secured of God's cunningness.

Never thought that God is cunning

Verse 166-When they ignored what they were forbidden, We said to them be scorned apes.

Why God condemns people this way?!

Verse 172-When your Lord took the descendants of the sons of Adam out of their loins, and made them witness to themselves, am I not your God, they said, yes we witness to say on the day of judgement we were ignorant about this.

Though some people think that children are conceived from their father's back but science completely refutes this.

Verse 176 – Had We wished We would have elevated him (man), but he preferred to be stuck to the ground & follow his desires. Its like a dog, if you threaten it, it pants, & if you leave it, it pants. That is like the people who falsify our statements. So tell them this story, so that they may reflect.

It is disgraceful to think of people who reject your teachings as panting dogs.

Verse 179 – We have assigned many jinn & people to hell. They have hearts with which they don't understand, they have eyes with which they do not see & they have ears with which they do not hear. They are more ignorant than cattle. They are the misguided.

Here again, why think of people who reject your teachings as ignorant cattle?

Verse 183-They were told that I am very spiteful

I always thought that God is very forgiving and merciful

SURAT AL-ANFAL-8

Verse 12- God inspired the angels, I am with you, so secure those who believed. I will throw terror in the hearts of those who disbelieved. So smite their necks and cut off all their fingers.

Why resort to terror & violence in a heavenly message.

Verse 13-This is because they strived against God and his messenger, and whoever strives against God and his messenger will be severely punished.

Why does God & his messenger resort to such action?

Verse 15- O you who believe, if you come across the infidels in defiance, don't turn your backs to them.

Why always expect the worse of others as if waiting to do you harm. This only reflects your nature.

Verse 16-Whoever on that day turns his back, unless in a manner of fighting, or swerving towards an assemblage, will end up with vengeance from God. His refuge will be hell & what a terrible end.

Where is compassion which everyone seeks from heaven?

Verse 30-As to those who disbelieved, they are cunning to control you, or kill you, or get rid of you. They are cunning and God is cunning. God is the best of all in cunning.

This is an attribute to God which I find very offensive.

Verse 39-And fight them so that there will not be insurrection and all religion will be to God, If they are finished, God knows what they were doing.

Why always resort to fighting and not resolving things in an acceptable way.

Verse 41-Know that anything you take in plunder, one fifth is to God, his messenger, the relatives, the orphans, the poor & those on the road ; if you believed in God and what was descended to our servant when both met on the day of revelation. God is capable of everything.

Isn't it horrible that God and his Messenger ask for a share of the plundering?!

Verse 60-And prepare for them all the force you can with saddled horses, terrorising with them the enemies of God and your enemies.and others whom you don't know, God knows them. What you spend for the sake of God will be given back to you and you will not be mistreated.

This is an obvious call from the almighty God for war and violence on his behalf.

Verse 65-O you prophet, entice the people to fight. If there are twenty of you persevering they will overcome two hundred, And if there are a hundred of you, they will overcome a thousand of those who disbelieved, for they don't understand.

What a terrible way to prepare people for holy war

Verse 66-God has lightened it for you, knowing your weakness. If there are a hundred of you persevering, they overcome two hundred, if there are a thousand of you, they overcome two thousand, God willing. God is with those who persevere.

The prophet realising he was asking too much of his followers as stated in the previous verse 65.

There is something weird about this verse 66. If the Qur'an is the book from heaven and everything in it is the word of God then why verse 66 starts with "God has lightened it for you ". It should be "I have lightened it for you". Otherwise who is the author?!!!

Verse 67-A prophet should not have prisoners until the land is tamed. You want the wealth of the world & God wants for you the afterlife. God is dear & wise.

Is killing better than taking prisoners?!

Verse 68-Had it not been previously written for what you have taken, you would have been severely tortured.

I expect completely the opposite. People should be punished after they have been shown what is supposedly the true path.

Verse 69-Eat and enjoy what you have lawfully taken by plundering. Fear God because God is forgiving & merciful.

How can any sane person enjoy what was plundered.

SURAT AL-TAUBAH -9

Verse 5-When the prohibited month ends, kill the heathens wherever you find them., Take them, surround them & lie in wait for them. If they repent & settle for prayer & give to charity, then let them go. God is forgiving & merciful.

Why this animosity towards the heathens. Let people believe what they want.

Verse 12-If they desecrate their faith after giving their pledge and deride your religion,, so fight the leaders of the infidels. They have no faith & they may be suppressed.

Resorting to violence again

Verse 13-Wouldn't you fight people who desecrate their faith & conspired to expel the messenger, & they were the first to start. Are you afraid of them. God is more worthy to be afraid of if you are believers.

Seeking revenge rather than reconciliation?

Verse 14-Fight them, God will torture them by your hands, will shame them & will make you victorious over them. This will get it off the chest of the believers.

Fighting to get this hatred off people's chests?! HOW AWFUL. It is unbelievable for God to say something like this in the Holy Qur'an.

Verse 23-O you who believed, do not take your fathers & your brothers as your superiors if they prefer infidelity to faith, those of you who do will be oppressors.

I cannot believe God is enticing people against members of their own family.? Let my father & my brother & the whole family believe what they want & I believe what I want. God will decide the fate of each of us after death, so if my family choose to end up in hell then that is their choice. So what is wrong taking them as my superiors.

Verse 28-O you who believed, the heathens are defiled, so they should not approach the sacred Mosque after this year.If you fear insufficiency, God will provide you from his favours if He wishes. God is Knowing & wise.

Why are the Heathens considered defiled?

Verse 29-Fight those who do not believe in God and the afterlife, and who do not prohibit what God & his messenger have prohibited, and they do not believe in the religion of truth amongst those who were sent the book (Jews & Christians), unless they give tribute with their hands subdued & they are despised.

Why should any people be looked at as despicable.

Verse 73-O you prophet, strive against the infidels & hypocrites, & be tough with them. Their refuge is hell & a terrible end.

Why this tenacious hatred towards the unbelievers. Where is compassion?

Verse 111-God has bought the believers themselves & their wealth so that they have heaven. They kill & get killed for the sake of God as truly promised in the Torah, the Bible & the Qur'an. Those who honour their promise with God, rejoice with the sale which you have concluded. That is the great victory.

God is asking people to provide whatever they have and get killed for his sake? If God created us to fight, kill & get killed, then what is His purpose creating us in the first place?!

Verse 113-It was not for the prophet & those who believed to forgive the heathens, even if they were next of kin, after it was apparent to them that they belonged to hell.

Enticing believers even against family members. I cannot be against my own family, no matter what.

Verse 123-O you who believed, fight those infidels who are around you, so that they find toughness in you & realise that God is with the pious.

Yet again no sympathy or kindness in what is supposed to be a heavenly book with divine teachings of peace, tolerance, forgiveness and compassion.

What I find confusing is that God asks His followers to do all these atrocities on His behalf. Certainly God has the power to send His angels to do everything He asks us feeble human beings to do, yet, He abstains from doing that!. Isn't that weird.

SURAT -YOUNES-10

Verse 3-Your Lord is God who created the heavens & the earth in six days, then settled on the throne organising things. No mediator except after His permission. That is God your Lord, so worship him, you are reminded.

It is the first time I know that God has a throne!

Verse 21-If people taste mercy after being struck by harm, & think cunningly of our verses, say God is faster cunning, as our messengers write down what you are cunning.

I have always been taught that only the devil is cunning, but in the Qur'an it is God who is cunning.

SURAT HUD-11

Verse 7-And He(God) who created the heavens & the earth in six days, & His throne was on the waters, He probed who amongst you is best in deeds,& if you say we are resurrecting after death, those who disbelieved will say this is obvious witchcraft.

Now strangely enough God's throne is on the waters!

SURAT YUSOF-12

Verse 2-We (God)have sent you the Qur'an in Arabic so that you will be rational.

Why the Qur'an should be only in Arabic. People like me would not understand a thing of what it says unless one studies Arabic to get the true meaning of its verses.

    Is Arabic the only language spoken by God in heaven?!

SURAT AL-RA'D-13

Verse 2-God who elevated the heavens without columns that you can see, then He settled on the throne, and subdued the sun & the moon, each moving for a finite time..He organises things and regulates the events, so that you eventually believe in meeting Him.

Science teaches me that the sun is stationary, unless what the Qur'an meant to say (which I probably did not understand) is that its movement is part and parcel of our galaxy in the milky way?! However, if that is the case, then to mention that "each moving for a finite time" is wrong, because that specifies the sun & the moon movements in relation to earth, otherwise it should be the sun, the moon & earth each moving for a finite time in relation to each other within space. Moreover, if the Qur'an adds space & their movement in space into the equation then it should use the phrase, infinite time, & not finite time, particularly so because their combined movement in space is at an accelerated rate, so their speed is changing constantly.

Verse 42-He was cunning those who came before them, God is the most cunning of all.He knows what every soul wins, and the infidels will know for whom is the worse abode.

How come God is the most cunning of all?!!. Cunning is an extremely bad attribute to anyone, let alone God.

SURAT IBRAHEEM-14

Verse 4-We did not send messengers except those who speak the language of their own people in order to teach them the grace of God. God will enlighten whom He wishes and stray away whom He wishes. He is the dear and the wise.

If God enlightens whom He wishes & strays away whom He wishes then what are we human beings to do if it is God's choice. Why are we to blame if we get things wrong.?

SURAT AL-HIJR- 15

Verse 19 And We spread out the earth & laid on it mountains & We planted in it all things in balance

Here again the earth is round, not flat

SURAT AL-NAHL-16

Verse 58-If someone was told that he has a daughter his face remained black & he was saddened.

Isn't this racial discrimination? It gives the impression that black is a bad omen.

Verse 71-God has bestowed better sustenance to some of you compared to others, so those who were given more should not share their sustenance equally with their captives. Do they deny God's blessings.

Why would God bestow to some more than others, Is this fair?

Verse 93-Had God wanted, He would have made you all one nation, but He guides whom He wishes & lays astray whom He wishes. You will be asked about your deeds.

Why does God prefer some to others, & how people will be held accountable for their deeds if they are predestined in what they do?! Isn't this weird?!

Verse 106-The wrath of God & severe torture be upon those who openly & wholeheartedly deny God. The same will be on those who deny him after belief, except if they do it under compulsion, but they are true believers in their hearts.

Isn't that hypocritical, to declare what is not really in your hearts. Is this what God wants us to be?!

SURAT AL-ISRA'-17

Verse 44-The seven heavens & the earth and what is in them glorify Him (God). Everything glorifies His grace but you do not understand their glorification. He was wise & forgiving.

As far as I know there are no seven heavens, unless this is something which has not been scientifically discovered yet.

SURAT AL-KAHF-18

Verse 86-When he arrived at sunset, he saw the sun setting in a hot spring & he found there people as well. We said, O you double horned, either you torture them or do them well.

Scientifically this does not make sense at all. It is the first time I read that the sun sets in a hot spring.

SURAT TAHA-20

Verse 5-The most merciful settled on the throne

What kind of throne is it. Thrones are for kings and emperors.

Vers 53- He who made the earth like a spread out carpet and arranged in it paths for you & brought down water from heaven which resulted in pairs of various plants

The earth is round, not flat

Verse 113-Likewise we have sent it down to them an Arabic Qur'an & we elucidated through it all warnings so that they take notice or make them remember.

What about people who don't know Arabic at all?

SURAT AL ANBEA' -21

Verse 30 – Didn't those who disbelieved see that the heavens and the earth were one unit which we pulled apart & we made every living thing out of water. Will they not believe then

I cannot check the authenticity of this verse as it is part of the creation of the heavens & the earth, however it does not make any sense to me. Moreover it is the first time I know that all living things are made out of water. Had it mentioned that water is essential for all life on earth, it would have made a big difference.

SURAT AL-HAJ-22

Verse 16-Likewise We (God) sent it (the Qur'an) down in clear verses. God enlightens whom He wishes.

If God enlightens whom he wishes so what is my role as a believer?

Verse 65-Can't you see? God has tamed the earth for you & the ships sailing the sea by His command. He holds the sky not to fall on earth except with his permission. God is kind & merciful to people.

How does God hold the sky from falling on earth?

SURAT AL-MU'MINOUN-23

Verse 5-And those who are protective of their vaginas (keeping themselves virgins?)

What kind of a language is this in the Holy Qur'an? Why God did not use phrases such as, "women who avoid sexual relationships with men"

Verse 6-They are not to be blamed if it is (having sex) with their partners or who they own as captives.

Why is it free to abuse captives. Is it because they have no power to resist?

Verse 14-Then We (God) made the semen a blood clot & the blood clot a chew. which We transformed to bones, and we covered the bones with meat, of which We created a new being, so blessed is God the best creator.

This verse contradicts everything I learnt in biology at high school. I know that the fertilised egg (which is a combination of a sperm & the egg) becomes a mass of cells which in due course, changes to different parts of the body, including cartilage which eventually becomes bones. There is no blood clot and there are no bones which are then covered by meat.

  Moreover to say that God is the best creator gives an impression that there are many creators & God is actually the best amongst them.

Verse 86-Say, who is the Lord of the seven heavens and the Lord of the great throne.

Which seven heavens & which great throne?!

SURAT AL-NOUR-24

Verse 2-Whip a hundred whips each man and woman who commit adultery. Show them no sympathy if you are in God's religion, believe in God & the day of judgement. Let a group of believers watch their punishment.

Why shame & punish people like that even though adultery is with mutual consent, however, one can do whatever and whenever one wants with captives, which probably on many occasions is nothing short of rape, yet in this situation it is condoned by God, accordingly there is no whipping & no punishment.

SURAT AL-FURQAAN-25

Verse 59-The One (God) who created the heavens & the earth & what is in between in six days, then settled on the merciful throne. Ask about it an experienced person.

What is meant by the merciful throne & who would be experienced enough for us to enquire if all this is true. I was told that what is meant by this verse is the merciful God settled on the throne. If this is the case then it means that I a non-Arab can write Arabic better than God of the Qur'an who they claim is the best in Arabic language, because if I were to write this verse I would write it as follows:

"The One (merciful God) who created the heavens & the earth & what is in between in six days, then settled on the throne. Ask about it an experienced person ".

SURAT AL SHUARAA' -26

Verse 195 – In a perspicuous Arabic language

Why should it be only in Arabic

SURAT AL-NAML - 27

Verse 17-So Solomon was gathered and organised an army of jinn, people & birds.

First time ever I hear of an army of Jinn & birds?!

Verse 18-when they reached the valley of the ants, an ant said," O you ants, enter your hidings, or you will be squashed by Solomon's soldiers without you knowing".

Isn't this weird to know that ants can talk and avoid destruction.

Verse 19-So he (Solomon) smiled laughing at her speech and said "O Lord, advise me how to thank you for the grace which you bestowed on me and my parents, make me do what is good to please you. Allow me with your mercy to be amongst your best worshipers."

Isn't it weird for Solomon to understand the ants' language, if there is one that is, which I & most people have never heard of.

Verse 20-He (Solomon) assembled the birds & said "I don't see the Hoopoe. Is it amongst the absentees?"

Would the Hoopoe need permission to be absent?!

Verse 21-I will torture him most severely or will slay him unless he (the Hoopoe) gives me a good explanation.

Is this what one expects of a king and a bird?!

Verse 22-He (the Hoopoe) stayed not far & said "I have come across things which you don't know. I have come to you with good news from Saba' ".

Can the Hoopoe also speak & give important information?!

Verse 23-I (the Hoopoe) Found a woman ruling over them & she has a great throne.

This Hoopoe must have been one of a kind?!

Verse 24-I (the Hoopoe) found her and her people worshipping the sun, not God. Satan has organised everything for them & deviated them from the true path. They are misled.

This Hoopoe is certainly very observant. He must have been an excellent spy.

Verse 25-Wouldn't they worship God who reveals what is hidden in the heavens and earth, & who knows what you hide and what you declare.

It is amazing. This Hoopoe is a great thinker & gives words of wisdom?!

Verse 26-God, there is no God but Him, Lord of the great throne.

Even the Hoopoe declares that there is only one God. What a perfect Hoopoe?!

Verse 27-(Solomon) said," we will see if you say the truth or telling lies ".

After all the Hoopoe has been through as a spying scout, risking his life in case he got caught in the act, we find king Solomon doubting what his spying scout is saying. Is this fair?!

Verse 28-Go with a letter of mine [king Solomon instructing the Hoopoe], deliver it to them & leave them. We will see what they come back with.

The Hoopoe proved to be the best none human messenger the world has ever seen.

Verse 39-A wicked jinn said, I will bring it (the throne of Saba') to you before you rise from your place. I am trustworthy & can do it.

The jinn is talking to king Solomon & reassuring him that he can conquer Saba'?!

I really wonder if anyone(ever since the Holy Qur'an was revealed to the most blessed prophet Mohammad) sought to find out the spiritual significance of this story of king Solomon, the speaking ant & the clever Hoopoe. There must certainly be a moral significance behind it which the feeble brain of us human beings cannot comprehend, otherwise such a story would never ever have been mentioned in one of the most important revelations to mankind. I also wonder, if only for argument sake, what would have happened if all the ants got squashed under the feet of the army & the Hoopoe was replaced by a human messenger. Would the end result have been the same?!

SURAT AL-ANKABOUT-29

Verse 21-He (God) tortures whom He pleases & saves whom He pleases. He decides.

It seems that we are predestined to what will eventually happen to us. God is not fair if this is the case.

Verse 62-God lays & increases the sustenance to whom He wishes amongst his followers. God is knowledgeable in everything

Why does God prefer some people to others? is this fair?

Verse 64-The life in this world is only entertainment and fun but the afterlife is the animal, had they known.

What does this verse really mean?? I suppose most probably it means care free life like the way animals live. However, when I enquired about the meaning of the word "animal" in this verse I was told that it means "life". If that is the case why didn't God use the word life instead of animal so that people understand his message without having to enquire about it. Did He intend to complicate matters for the reader of his message, I wonder?

SURAT LUQMAAN-31

Verse 19-Walk slowly and lower your voice, the worse sounds are those of donkeys.

Why such a verse comes from God in the Holy Qur'an & why the sounds of donkeys are the worse of all. Many people enjoy listening to donkeys when they bray.

SURAT AL SAJADAH-32

Verse 4-God who created the heavens & the earth & what is in between in six days, then settled on the throne. There is no one else superior or mediator to intercede to. Can't you realise.

Here again mentioning the throne. What kind of a throne is it?!

Verse 13-We could have given every soul its true guidance had We so wished, but verily my saying goes, I will fill up hell with jinn and people altogether.

I thought God is the most merciful & most forgiving, but here he wants to fill up hell with people & jinn.

SURAT AL-AHZAAB -33

Verse 1-O you prophet, fear God. Do not obey the infidels & the hypocrites. God was knowledgeable & wise.

If the Qur'an is the word of God then why is God using the past tense for knowledge & wisdom. It should have been stated "God is knowledgeable & wise". This means that God's mastering of the Arabic language is not very good. And He is not now knowledgeable & wise.

Verse 26-God brought down from the strongholds their supporters of the people of the Book. & threw terror in their hearts. Some of them you kill & others you take prisoners.

Why God is seeking violence?!

Verse 27-God made you heirs of their land, their properties & their possessions. A land which you have not stepped on previously. God was capable of everything.

God here condones plundering, which I find very strange indeed.

Verse 37-And you say to whoever God & you (the prophet Mohammad) have given grace, keep your wife & fear God. You hide your feelings of what God is giving you because you are afraid of people, yet it is God whom you should be afraid of. When Zaid (the prophet Muhammad's adopted son) had enough of her (Zaid's wife) We (God) have given her (Zaid's wife) to you(Muhammad), so that you would not be embarrassed amongst the believers. So they (the believers) can get married to the wives of their adopted sons once they (their adopted sons) have had enough of their wives. God's order is to be done.

I cannot believe God is allowing men to get married to the wives of their adopted sons.

Verse 40-Muhammad was not the father of any of your men, but a messenger of God & the last of the prophets. God was knowing everything.

Few men claimed to be prophets and have followers numbering hundreds of millions since prophet Mohammad's death. For example Joseph Smith in the USA & the Mormon Movement, Mirza Ghulam Ahmad in India who claimed to be the second Messiah. Dahesh Beig who has the Dahesh School and Movement starting in Palestine then moved to Lebanon, he died in the USA. He has a museum in his name & wrote many books. Baha'Uddeen from Pershia with the Bahai religion & movement. He died in Israel. So Muhammad definitely was not the last of the prophets.

    Moreover, yet again God is using past tense. Why not say" God Knows everything".

Verse 50-O you prophet, We (God) have authorised you wives whom you have paid their dowry & whoever you own of what God has given you as captives, & your female cousins on your mother's & father's sides who emigrated with you & a female believer who offers herself to the prophet if the prophet wants to have sexual intercourse with her. This is only for you, but not the believers. We knew what wives & captives were allotted to them so that you wouldn't be embarrassed. God was forgiving & merciful.

God provides sexual favours to the prophet, not for others.

    Also the use of past tense. Why not say "God is forgiving & merciful ".

Verse 51-You defer whom you wish amongst them, keep whom you wish & whoever of those you abandoned. You will not be blamed. That is the least to please their eyes & not be sorrowful, yet accepting for what you have given them. God knows what is in their hearts. God is Knowledgeable & wise.

More favours from God to the prophet

Verse 56-God & the angels pray for the prophet. O you who believe, pray for him & greet him abundantly.

First time I know that God prays for the prophet. That is extremely weird?!

Verse 57-Those who do harm to God & His messenger, God has cursed them in this world & thereafter, and has prepared for them a humiliating torture.

Why would God prepare torture to those who do harm to his messenger. What if they repent afterwards?

Verse 61-Cursed be wherever they are. They are to be taken, killed & butchered.

For heaven's sake, why resort to such violence In the Holy Qur'an.

Verse 64-God has cursed the infidels & prepared for them inferno

Why God's hatred in the Qur'an is so unforgiving, yet throughout the Qur'an one reads "God, the most merciful & the most forgiving ". It is absolutely contradictory.

SURAT SABA'-34

Verse 36-Say that my God makes it easy to provide to whom He wishes & He can do that, but most people don't know.

Why doesn't God provide equally to everyone?!

Verse 39-Say that my God makes it easy to provide to whom He wishes amongst his worshipers. He can do that & whatever you spend he will replace it for you. He is the best provider.

Why doesn't God provide equally to everyone as well. Why does He prefer some to others?!

SURAT FATER-35

Verse 8-He whose bad deed was looked at favourably & he thought it good, it is God who strays whom He wishes & guides whom He wishes, so don't let yourself pity them. God knows what they are doing.

Why does the ever loving God lead people astray?!

Verse 33-They enter the Garden of Eden where they will be embellished with gold bracelets & pearl with silk dresses.

I never ever thought that such items are available or even exist in the Garden of Eden. These are worldly things.

SURAT YASEEN-36

Verse 38-And the sun moves to its resting place, that is the estimate of the knowledgeable dear.

Science tells me that the sun does not move (except if the Qur'an means its movement as part of the galaxy it is in, but even so, it has no place for it to rest).

Verse 56-They and their wives reclining on sofas in the shade.

This gives the impression that people are married in heaven. That there is sun & it is somewhat hot in order to sit lazily on sofas in the shade.

Verse 57-They have in it fruits & whatever they want.

The Garden of Eden looks like a real fruit garden in the Holy Qur'an.

SURAT AL SAFFAAT-37

Verse 125-You call upon Ba'l & you abandon the best creator

Does this verse in the Qur'an mean there are other creators but God of the Qur'an is the best amongst them?!

SURAT AL-ZUMAR-39

Verse 20-But those who feared God will have rooms with rooms built on top, & rivers flowing underneath. This was God's promise & He does not fail in His promise.

I never thought there are multi-storey buildings with rivers in heaven. I wonder if these rooms are made of brick & mortar, steel, wood, a combination of these, or some other heavenly material we don't know about.

Verse 28-An Arabic Qur'an without crookedness so that they be guided.

Why does it have to be Arabic & not any other language to guide other people as well. This is very discriminatory to non-Arabs.

Verse 52-Don't they understand that God provides easily to whom he wishes & can do that. That on its own is a sign to people who believe.

Why does God have preferences as to whom He provides to?!

Verse 60-You will see on the day of judgement those who lied to God. Their faces are blackened, isn't hell an abode for the proud.

Again racial discrimination against blacks. Why didn't God say their faces will be white with shame & fear as an example. I say this because when people get afraid or very sick the colour of their faces turns white like a white sheet as it gets drained of its blood. Yet God has intentionally used the black colour to describe the people in hell.

Verse 73-And those who feared God were led in groups to the garden, & when they arrived, its gates opened. The gatekeeper greeted them "peace be upon you, you have done well, so enter for ever ".

Isn't it strange to have a garden with gates & a gatekeeper in heaven?! Is it also in heaven that there are bandits whom we should fear & be protected from them?!

SURAT FUSSILAT-41

Verse 3-Well arranged verses in an Arabic Qur'an Book for people who understand.

What about people who don't understand, especially those who do not understand Arabic?!

Verse 12-He (God) completed the seven heavens in two days & assigned to each heaven its duty. He adorned the lowermost with lamps & guarded it. That is the arrangement of the knowledgeable dear.

I know there is only one heaven, unless I am scientifically wrong.

SURAT AL-SHURA-42

Verse 8-Had God wished He would have made them one people but He admits whoever He wishes to his mercy. The oppressors have no protector and no supporter.

God is discriminating people from each other.

Verse 13-You have been given of religion what already was ordered through Noah & through you (Muhammad). Also what we ordered through Abraham, Moses & Issa to establish religion without deviation in it, otherwise what you call for, will be difficult for those who are polytheists. God attracts to Him whom He wishes & guides those who look for others (other gods).

I always thought that God attracts to Him every body.

Verse 19-God is kind to his worshipers. He provides to whom He wishes. He is the strong & dear.

Why does God provide only to whom He wishes. What about the others.

Verse 50-He weds them male & female & He makes infertile whom he wishes. He is knowledgeable and capable.

Why on earth would God make people willingly infertile. I cannot comprehend a God who intentionally does this kind of thing. This is awful to say the least.

Qur'an Verses which stopped a Judeo- Christian converting to Islam

Verse 52-Likewise We (God) have inspired you a spirit through our command. You didn't know about the book or the faith but We (God) made it a light to guide through it whoever We (God) wish of our worshipers. you guide people to the true path.

Why guide only who God wishes, what about the others.

SURAT AL-ZUKHROF-43

Verse 3 – We made it an Arabic Qur'an so that you rationalise.

Why only Arabic Qur'an. What about people who do not understand Arabic.

Verse 10 – He who made the earth like spread out carpet with paths in it that you may be guided

My understanding is that the earth is round, not flat

Verse 71-Golden dishes & goblets full of what the soul desires & pleases the eye will be passed around. You last in it for ever.

I never thought these things exist in heaven?!

Verse 72-That is the garden which we (God) made you heir of as you were told.

A very worldly garden indeed, fortunately lasting for ever.

Verse 73-You have in it many fruits which you can eat.

Are the fruits different to what is available here on earth?! I just wonder.

SURAT AL-DUKHAAN-44

Verse 52-In gardens & springs.

We have gardens & springs here on earth as well, are those in heaven different?!

Verse 53-Facing each other dressing silk & brocade.

As if preparing for a grand occasion or a party?!.

Verse 54-Likewise we wed them to white eyed women.

I never thought that souls get married in the afterlife. Incidentally, do women get married in heaven to white eyed men as well?!

Verse 55-They ask for any fruit, knowing it is secured.

What a great way to end in heaven with everlasting fruits.

SURAT MUHAMMAD-47

Verse 4-If you come across those who disbelieved, strike their necks (behead them), once subdued, tie them up firmly, either for us later or for ransom until war cools down. If God wishes He will win over them, but you dispute amongst ourselves. Those who got killed for the sake of God their deed will not be in vain.

Why always fighting the infidels and seek such violence by God?!.

Verse 15-Like the garden they were promised. It has rivers of clear water, rivers of milk whose taste does not change, rivers of wine delicious to whoever drinks from them, rivers of pure honey & all kinds of fruits with blessings from God, unlike those who are in everlasting fire, drinking hot water which cuts their bowels.

Very imaginative garden indeed compared to hell?

Verse 35-Don't weaken & ask for peace when you are dominant. God is with you, He wouldn't lessen your deeds.

Isn't it the best time to ask for peace when you are dominant to avoid further violence. God seems to be very unforgiving & likes subduing people by violence.

SURAT AL-FATH-48

Verse 9-So that you believe in God & His messenger, & support him, respect him & bless him morning and evening.

Why do all of that for the messenger, after all, he is a human being like the rest of us but with supposedly a message from God.

Verse 14-The heavens & the earth belong to God. He forgives whom He wishes and tortures whom He wishes. God was forgiving and merciful.

Why God chooses whom to forgive & torture. Moreover, if God was forgiving & merciful, is He still forgiving & merciful, I wonder?!

Verse 16 – Say to deserters amongst the Arabs, you will be called upon against very tough people. You fight them or they submit. If they obey, God will grant you a good reward. If you abandon as you did before, God will punish you severely.

God punishes people who do not fight for his sake?!

SURAT AL-HUJURAAT-49

Verse 9-If two parties amongst the believers fight with each other reconcile them. If one party transgresses against the other, fight the transgressors until they comply with God's orders. If they do, make just peace between them. God loves fair people.

Why fight the transgressors & not use some other peaceful means first. It is very strange that throughout the Qur'an violence is the first means of sorting things out.

SURAT QAF -50

Verse 7 – We have spread out the earth and laid on it mountains & planted in it of all beautiful pairs

Here again the earth is round, not flat

SURAT AL-THAREAAT -51

Verse 48 – And the earth was flattened, how good are the planners

The earth is round, not flat

Verse 49 – We have created pairs out of all things, so that you take notice

This is not true at all. My studies in biology at high school taught me that there are many hermaphrodite creatures with male & female sexual organs in the same creature. Also there are creatures that divide into two separate creatures & multiply in this way without any sexual organs. So, not every creature needs to be in pairs to reproduce.

SURAT AL-TOUR-52

Verse 20-Reclining on prepared beds & we wed them to white eyed(women).

Yet again I am really getting confused about this wedding business in heaven?!

Verse 22-And we provided them with fruits & what they desire of meat.

They eat & drink in heaven yet nothing is mentioned about them sweating, urinating & defecating? Are there bathrooms (rest rooms, toilets), showers & all the other facilities, I just wonder?!.

Verse 23-Exchanging cups without trifling or deriding.

Having cups full of drinks as well?!

Verse 24-Young boys like perfect pearls go around serving them.

Why have young boys & not angels. This is absolutely weird?! Is the intention here some kind of molestation or what?! I am baffled?!

SURAT AL-WAAQIA'H-56

Verse 15-On beds embossed with precious stones.

Is this actually in heaven?!

Verse 16-Reclining on it, opposite each other.

What does this mean? Is it to give the feeling of complete relaxation, I wonder.

Verse 17-Being served round by everlasting young boys.

Boys again, why not angels?!

Verse 18-With goblets, beakers & cups of clear spring water.

Is this a party with servants?!

Verse 20-And fruits of whatever they chose.

Are there all kinds of fruit trees in heaven?!

Verse 21-And birds meat whatever they desire.

Do they eat it raw?!. Otherwise who does the cooking, is it the boys?, the angels?, the white eyed women?, the men themselves?, or are there special cooks already prepared by God or what? Incidentally, is there a kitchen? & if so, who cleans the dishes & utensils?I wonder?!

Verse22-And white eyed (women).

Are these women for sexual entertainment, what is their function?!

Verse23-Like perfect pearl

What is so special about pearl?

Verse 28-In a yard of thorn-less trees.

Is this in heaven?

Verse 29-Plants on top of each other.

Also this in heaven?

Verse 30-Extended shade.

Does the sun shine there as well?

Verse 31-And flowing water

Do they get thirsty in heaven?

Verse 32-And plenty of fruits.

It seems the fruits in heaven are never ending.

Verse 34-And raised beds

Do they actually sleep in heaven? I wonder if there is daytime & night time. Do they get siestas in the afternoon. It seems there are lots of things in heaven that we don't know about.

Verse 36-We (God) made them virgins.

Why do they need virgin women in heaven?! And why would God get involved in this trivial matter in the Holy Qur'an?!

SURAT AL HADEED-57

Verse 10-Why don't you spend for the sake of God & He owns the heavens & the earth. Those of you who spent & fought before we waged war will be rewarded better than those who spent & fought afterwards. God promised to reward both. God knows what you do.

God rewards better those who spent & fought from the beginning rather than those who joined later. What about those who never heard till later about what God wants?

SURAR AL-MUJADILAH-58

Verse 22-You will not find people who believe in God & the afterlife having good relationship with those who oppose God & His messenger, even if they were their fathers, sons, brothers or tribe.God wrote in their hearts the belief and empowered them with His spirit. He (God) will admit them to gardens with flowing rivers underneath, to live there forever. God is pleased with them and they are pleased with Him. Those are the party of God & the party of God are the winners.

I find this verse completely incomprehensible, divisive, incredible, unethical and inexplicable in the Holy Qur'an. How does God expect me to be against my own family even if they believe whatever they want to believe. Let God deal with them after death the way He wants. Why create hatred and animosity between me & my family. Yet in the Qur'an Surat Al-Kafiroun 109 Verse 6 it says "You have your religion & I have mine". What a contradiction?!

    I believe God wants us to love each other, not to hate each other, if He is a fair loving God.

SURAT AL-HASHR-59

Verse 23-He is God, there is no God but Him, the holy king, the peace maker, the believer, the controller, the dear, the mighty, the proud. Glory be to God not for what polytheists believe.

I find pride somewhat an unacceptable tribute to God. Moreover God is "the believer" in what?!

SURAT ALMUMTAHANAH-60

Verse 1-O you who believed, don't take my enemies & your enemies as your superiors & show them affection, yet they disregarded the truth that was given to you. They expelled you & the messenger for believing in God. If you have been driven out & strived for my sake to please me then don't be friendly with them.I know what you concealed & what you revealed. Any of you who does that has strayed the straight path.

God shows very clearly His intolerance of other people.

Verse 10 - O you who believed, if female believers emigrate to you, check them out. God knows their faith. If you find them believers, don't send them back to the infidels, they are not lawful to their husbands & their husbands are not lawful to them. Give them what they have spent & you are not blamed if you have sexual intercourse with them, providing you pay them what is due. Don't hold on to them. Ask what you have spent & let them ask what they have spent. That is God's judgement & He judges between you. God is Knowledgeable and wise.

God allowing sexual favours for money, isn't that weird?!

SURAT AL-SAFF-61

Verse 4-God loves those who fight for His cause in rows like a united structure.

God loves people who fight for Him???

SURAT AL-JUMUAT - 62

Verse 5 – Its like those who were conveyed the Torah, then did not abide by it, is like a donkey burdened by books. Its like miserable people who deny the teachings of God. He does not guide the oppressors.

Why think of people as donkeys?! Would you like these same people to think of you as a donkey if you don't follow their own teachings.

SURAT AL-TALAAQ -65

Verse 4 – Those amongst your women whose periods have ceased & you are doubtful about them being pregnant, give them three months grace. Those whose periods have not yet started & they are pregnant wait until their pregnancy is over. God simplifies problems for those who fear him

I find this verse absolutely shocking, Never expected God to condone sexual activity with young girls whose periods have not yet started.

Verse 12 – God who created seven heavens and likewise with earth. He descends his command in between so that you know that God is capable of everything, and He has comprehensive knowledge in all things.

This is the first time I know that there are seven heavens and likewise seven earths. Our great stride in the understanding of the universe, and our ability to see distant galaxies millions of light years away, deep in space, which we call the heavens, failed to show us a second heaven or earth, let alone a third or a fourth or a fifth or a sixth or a seventh heaven or earth. As far as I am concerned this is all a scientific nonsense.

SURAT AL-TAHREEM-66

Verse 9-O you prophet, strive against the infidels & hypocrites. Be firm with them. Their abode is hell & a terrible end.

Why not talk to the infidels & hypocrites & convince them about the true faith.

Verse 12-And Mariam the daughter of Imran who maintained her virginity, we (God) breathed of our soul into her vagina. She believed in her Lord's words & books. She was devout

I cannot believe such language being mentioned in the Holy Qur'an. I also cannot believe in a God blowing his spirit in Mary's vagina?! Why didn't He choose her mouth or nose or ear or implant His soul in her from a distance. It is very, very, very weird for God who has the power to do anything to choose the vagina out of all other places.

My studies in Arabic taught me that the word (daughter, IBNAT in Arabic should be with a closed "T" "ة" at the end, not the long flat "T" "ت". So this is an Arabic spelling mistake of a supposedly everlasting divine revelation written by the Supreme God without any fault or deviation whatsoever. It so happens that a non-Arab like me has to correct His Arabic language.

SURAT AL-MULK-67

Verse 3-(God) who created seven heavens in layers. You don't see in the creation of the merciful any deviation. Look again, do you see any fault.

Never heard of seven heavens on top of each other before. Has science confirmed this. I might be totally ignorant about these scientific issues as it is not my field of education. May be the Holy Qur'an is mentioning things that have not been discovered to date. However, in the verse it says "look again, do you see any fault". This means that we should be able to see it. I am just baffled???!!!

Verse 5-And we decorated the lowermost heaven with lamps to shoot the Satan/s. We (God) have prepared for them severe torture.

Isn't it weird that the stars we see in the sky at night are used as missiles to beat the devils with them. I understand that the number of stars is absolutely huge. All one has to do is sit & count the number of stars in a cloudless sky at night, probably your life will end before you finish counting the stars in the only patch which is visible to you. Does this mean that there is a huge number of Satan/s or there is a huge number of stars assigned per Satan or what???!!! Can someone answer this very intriguing phenomena.

SURAT AL-MA'AREJ-70

Verse 29-And those who protect their vaginas (maintain their virginity).

Is this a language to use in a Holy Qur'an? Why not use a language similar to what is in between the brackets. There is something equal to that in Arabic.

I don't understand the Holy Qur'an at times with its use of vulgar language on many occasions. It is as if God is very sexually oriented, or His choice of the most proper words in Arabic is limited.

Verse 30-Except to their partners (husbands) or what they (husbands) own as captives. They are not to be blamed.

Verse 30 is a continuation of verse 29. Basically it means that women should not have intercourse except with their husbands, and their husbands can also have intercourse with their captives.

Isn't it terrible that captives are considered for men's sexual pleasure whenever they wish?!

SURAT NOUH-71

Verse 15-Can't you see how God created seven heavens in layers.

Here we go again, seven heavens on top of each other. Can someone please look into this & check if it is fact or fiction because I am not scientifically oriented.

Verse 19 – And God made the earth a spread out carpet for you

Another verse which indicates the earth is flat, not round

SURAT AL-MUZAMMEL-73

Verse 20- "fighting for the sake of God"

This is a phrase quoted out of verse 20. I just want to comment why people should fight for the sake of God. Fighting & violence seem to be a constant theme in the Holy Qur'an. Only one angel from God can do everything that the Holy Qur'an is requesting people to do on this earth. Am I missing something about the nature of God & every thing that can be done through Him. So why is God asking us human beings to do everything including fighting, beheading, slaughtering, butchering & torturing on his behalf.?!

SURAT ALMUDDATHTHER-74

Verse 31-"Likewise God strays whom He wishes & guides whom He wishes"

This is a phrase quoted out of verse 31. I just want to comment, why is it that God differentiates between people the way He wishes, Don't you think that all human beings should be looked at equally & each be treated according to his/her deeds? Sometimes I get the feeling from the Holy Qur'an that God is not fair at all. He should guide everyone, not only those whom He wishes.

SURAT AL-INSAAN-76

Verse 12-They were rewarded for their patience a garden & silk

A garden & silk in heaven? Who maintains the garden & weaves the silk?

Verse 13-Reclining on sofas, not seeing the sun or blustering weather.

Very things we experience on earth!

Verse 14-Its shadows getting close to them & the bunches (grapes) are really low.

Looks very serene, similar to Napa Valley in California.

Verse 15-(Boys) going round to them with silver saucers & goblets that were jars.

Very lavish and earthly.

Verse 16-Jars of silver to their estimate.

Precious items in heaven.??

Verse 17-They were given a cup of zangabeel to drink.

A very tasty drink in heaven.

Verse 18-A spring there called Salsabeel.

Fountains in heaven as well?!

Verse 19-Young everlasting boys go around them & when you see them you think they are spread pearls.

What is this depiction of young boys. There is certainly some form of sexual insinuation here, & if that is the case, it would be absolutely disgusting to think of young boys in this way, especially being mentioned in the Holy Qur'an & condoned by God the most sacred, the fairest & the most loving.

Verse 20-And when you look you will see bliss & a big realm.

Is this the prediction of what heaven is like?

Verse 21-They have on them green silk clothes with brocade & beautiful silver bracelets & God gave them tasty drinks.

Wow, all of this splendour in heaven with God handing us tasty drinks?!

SURAR AL-NAZIAAT -79

Verse 30 After that He flattened and spread out the earth

Again, the earth is round, not flat

SURAT AL-MASSAD-111

Verse 1-Perish the hands of Abi Lahab.

Why wish bad things for someone in the Holy Qur'an.

Verse 3-He will be burnt with flaming fire

Why wish this as well to whoever it may be. Why not say, may God forgive you for what you have done or said or whatever.

Verse 4-And his wife who carries logs of wood.

I find it strange that God would demean a woman for carrying wood. [I was told however, that the wood she was carrying was meant to burn her husband with it]

When I enquired about this" Surat ", I was told that Abi Lahab was prophet Muhammad's uncle who did not believe in the prophet's mission. God was upset that His messenger was ridiculed by his uncle openly in front of many people. As a result of this, God decided to include a "Surat" in the Holy Qur'an to punish Abi Lahab & his wife.

I find this extremely weird to say the least. Why would God get involved in something as trivial as this in His revelation to the Prophet. It is an incident which in my humble opinion should not have been mentioned at all in the Holy Qur'an. It is normal for prophets to be ridiculed by their own people. It is not easy to convey a new divine message to people, whoever and wherever they are.

CONCLUSION

My final impression of my reading the Holy Qur'an in bullet points :

1 – It contains lots of repetitions, God could have condensed it to at least half of its current volume without losing any of its intended content. For example, Surat Al-Kafiroun -109 Verse 2 to verse 5 say exactly the same thing but in different wordings:

> Verse 2 – I do not worship what you worship.
> Verse 3 _ And you are not worshiping what I worship.
> Verse 4 _ And I am not worshiping what you worshiped.
> Verse 5 _ And you are not worshiping what I worship.

2 - Some verses do not make any sense at all, for example : Surat Al-Teen 95 :

> Verse 1 – And the figs and the olives.
> Verse 2 – And mount Sinai.
> Verse 3 – And this secure country.
> All these verses have nothing to do with the rest of the Surah

3 – Few verses are difficult to understand what they mean, for example Surat Al-Ikhlaas 112 Verse 2 God the" Samad ""صمدُ"". I asked my good friend what does this word mean but he did not know. So when we were at the Mosque we asked a couple of worshipers what is the meaning of this word. I was given different answers. One said, it means" straight", another said, it means "dominant" and a third said, it means "persevering". So with no two same answers we decided to ask the Imam of

the Mosque what the word" Samad" means. He said it means "eternal ". Then I thought to myself if it means eternal why didn't it say so in a plain Arabic word "AL- ABADI". So really I was not convinced of that interpretation & I still don't know what that word means.

4 – Many verses & sometimes Suwar (plural of Surah/Surat) do not have any spiritual meaning : for example Surat Al-Feel 105

> Verse 1 – Can't you see what your God has done to the owners of the Feel (Elephant).
> Verse 2 – Didn't He astray their cunning.
> Verse 3 – And He send them flocks of birds.
> Verse 4 – Throwing at them stones of baked clay.
> Verse 5 – And He made them like an eaten up field.
> Can any one honestly ask himself/ herself what this whole Surah means spiritually & why is it in the Holy Qur'an? & what is its significance?

5 – There are many verses in the Qur'an full of sexual references. A number of these have been mentioned throughout this book. There is no point in enumerating them.

6 – Occasional phrases & words have, in my opinion, no place for them being in the Holy Qur'an, such as sexual intercourse (Nikaah) & vagina (Farj).

7 – It is full of contradictions. There are many verses that ask for peace, forgiveness & compassion, yet, other verses incite fighting, killing, beheading, torture …etc.

8 – It contains spelling & other Arabic language mistakes, yet it is supposed to be the top book in the Arabic language. For example, the use of past for present tense & vice versa & words ending with "T" sometimes it is written "t" & vice versa "ة\ت".

I am absolutely certain that an Arabic language scholar can find many grammatical mistakes which are not obvious to me.

9 – I got the feeling that rhyme & poetic flow is much more important than accuracy of the Arabic language in the Holy Qur'an. I must admit that I enjoyed this attribute while I was reading it.

!0 – Well known verses completely contradict established science in every sense of the word. I have mentioned a few throughout the text & there is no need to go through them again.

11 – It is the most disorganised book I ever read, for example, the story of the prophet Moses is written here & there in various Suwar (plural of Surah/Surat).

One can hardly read the story of anything which will be confined to one chapter or (Surah/Surat). It is like having a metallic item which consists of many parts, each part is hidden underground in a different area (chapter) of a field (book), then you go with a metal detector searching for each part separately in order to assemble the whole item.

12 – It is also the most confusing book I ever read. It says something, then advises on something else. For example, There are verses in the Holy Qur'an referring to Issa(Christ) as the word & the spirit of God. It also mentions that he spoke in infancy, created a bird out of shaped mud, healed the lepers & resurrected the dead. Surely, the word & spirit of God who could do all these things is God himself. If this is the case, then Issa(Christ) being God must be superior to his messenger the prophet Muhammad. but, the Quran refers to Issa (Christ) as another past messenger inferior in his qualities to Muhammad [who incidentally did nothing at all similar to Issa (Christ) despite the people begging him to show them at least one miracle].

13 – It is sometimes difficult to say who actually wrote the Holy Qur'an. Many verses start by" God" asks you to do this & that, while it really should be "I" ask you to do this & that. I could dig out many verses which very clearly show it was not God who wrote those verses.Take this verse as a good example, Surat Al-Imraan 3 Verse 169: "Do not think that those who got killed for the sake of God are dead, they are alive and doing well with God". If it is God who actually wrote this verse it would read like "Do not think that those who got killed for my sake are dead, they are alive and doing well with me."

I can very easily pick up many verses like this one & explain them to you.

!4 – There were verses in the Qur'an with blatant racial discrimination against black people, the content of these verses is abhorrent.

15 – It seems that many Moslems don't know much about the content of the Holy Qur'an. When I enquired about certain things in it they looked bewildered & they couldn't answer my questions. When I told them what I read, they thought I was making things up. On many occasions I just shut up or said to them go and check it up yourselves, but make sure you read it with an open mind.

16 – Some verses do not make any sense at all for an adult, but might be very entertaining for children. May be that is why they are mentioned, to encourage children to read the Holy Qur'an, for example the verse stating that the stars are used as missiles to beat the devil/s with them.

!7 – There are verses whose interpretations are very controversial. For example, the verses which deal about the creation & whether God created the earth flat or round. I have listed a number of these verses in this book, which, if interpreted as they are written, actually mean that the earth is flat. These verses are :

　　2/22
　　15/19
　　20/53
　　43/10
　　50/7
　　51/48
　　71/19
　　79/30

However, admittedly, I have learnt recently that the word "earth" in Arabic could mean our(earth/world) that we live on, or it could also mean a piece of land. Some Moslems who tried to answer my queries about these verses did not know if the word earth means the world we live on or a piece of land. I personally think the word earth in these verses means our world. it is up to the reader to agree or disagree with my interpretation.

18 – A few verses have very debatable interpretations, for example, verse 21/30 which states that the earth & the heavens (which basically means our earth & the whole universe) were in the beginning as one unit which were later separated by God to what we see now.Unless some one was there at the time to see if that was the case or has the scientific knowledge to prove it, then no one can refute this. I discussed this point with my good Moslem friend, he was adamant that this is actually the Islamic interpretation of the Big Bang Theory that astronomers & scientists have been talking about recently. There was no way I could argue with him that the Islamic interpretation is not really what the Big Bang Theory says. Our discussion ended no where.

I must admit it is not easy at all to convince someone of something contrary to what he/she has been indoctrinated since childhood.

Probably, I am in the same boat, having been indoctrinated throughout my life in a Judeo-Christian environment and all of a sudden trying to convert to a religion that I knew nothing about with the fear of the unknown. I must say though, my father's advice "never let your heart rule over your mind" keeps always ringing in my ears. He said to me if you follow this advice you will always prosper.

19 – Had it not been for the rhyme and poetic flow of the verses in the Holy Qur'an I would have said it was the most punishing and boring book to read

20 – I have read many books in my life, the Holy Qur'an was the only book in which God incites, encourages and asks his believers to kill others who do not want to believe in Him. To my knowledge there is no other book (religious or non-religious) that requests human beings to kill innocent people if they don't toe the line and follow the teachings of that book.

21 – Finally, I hope this book will help those who want to convert to Islam to decide which path to take. Best of luck to them, whatever is their decision.

20 - لقد قرأت كثيراً من الكتب في حياتي وكان القرآن الكريم ؟؟؟!!! الكتاب الوحيد الذي يحث فيه الله تابعيه قتل الآخرين الذين لا يريدون الإيمان به . كما لا أعلم لا يوجد كتاب آخر (ديني أو غير ديني) يطالب الناس بقتل أبرياء لأنهم يرفضون تعاليمهم وما جاء في كتبهم

21 - ختاماً - أملي أن يكون هذا الكتاب مفيداً للراغبين في التحول إلى الإسلام لكي يتمكنوا أن يختاروا الطريق الذي يرغبون في اتخاذه وأتمنى للجميع بالحظ السعيد أياً كان قرارهم .

51/48
71/19
79/30

وللحقيقة علمت مؤخراً أن الأرض باللغة العربية تعني الكرة الأرضية التي نعيش عليها وقد تعني أيضاً اي قطعة أرض . بعض المسلمين الذين سألتهم عن معنى هذه الآيات لم يعرفوا إذا معناها الكرة الأرضية أم قطعة أرض . أنا أعتقد أن المعنى هو الكرة الأرضية وليس قطعة أرض وعلى القارىء أن يفسرها كما يشاء .

18 - هنالك بعض الآيات قابلة للجدل في تفسيرها , مثالاً آية 21/30 التي تنص أن الأرض والسماوات كانت في البدء وحدة واحدة وأن الله فصلهما عن بعضهما فيما بعد لما نراه اليوم . بالطبع من الصعب نقد هذه الآية إلا إذا كان أحداً موجوداً ليراها عندما حدثت أو أنه من الممكن إثباتها علمياً , ولما بحثت هذه الآية مع صديقي أصر أن هذا هو التفسير الإسلامي للانفجار الكبير الذي تكلموا عنه العلماء وأخصائيي الفضاء مؤخراً , وكان من المستحيل إقناعه بأن التفاسير الإسلامية لا تمت بأي صلة للانفجار الكبير . وفي النهاية انتهى حديثنا بدون جدوى. يجب علي أن أقر أنه من الصعب جداً تغيير مبدأ تشرب عليه الإنسان منذ طفولته . ولا شك أن هذا ينطبق علي أيضاً لما تشربت به طيلة حياتي في محيط يهودي ومسيحي وفجأة اريد أن التحق إلى دين آخر لا اعرف عنه اي شيء والخوف من المجهول . ولكنني أفصح القول بنصيحة والدي " لا تجعل قلبك يحكم عقلك أبداً" ترن في أذني باستمرار . وقال لي إذا اتبعت هذه النصيحة يحالفك النجاح على الدوام .

19 – لو لم يكن القرآن مليء بالسجع وأسلوبه الشعري بالقافية لقلت عنه أنه أكثر كتاب ممل يعاقب قارئه في قرائته

الله هو الذي كتب هذا لكان يجب أن تُقرأ هكذا " ولا تحسبن الذين قتلوا من أجلي أمواتا بل هم أحياء عندي يرزقون " باستطاعتي أن أنتقي كثيراً من الآيات المشابهة وافسرها للقارىء

14 — هناك آيات في القرآن تحتوي على تفرقة عنصرية صارخة تجاه ذوي البشرة السوداء

15 — الظاهر أن كثيراً من المسلمين لا يعرفون محتوى القرآن الكريم لأنني عندما كنت أسألهم عن أشياء فيه كانوا ينظرون لي باستغراب ولم يعرفوا الإجابة على أسئلتي . وعندما قلت لهم هذا ما قرأته اعتقدوا أن ما كنت اقوله كان ما من صنع خيالي . وكثيراً من الأحيان كنت أقول لهم ابحثوا الأمور بأنفسكم ولكن بعقول مفتوحة

16 — بعض الآيات ليس لها معنى إطلاقاً للشخص العاقل ولكنها تجذب الأطفال لقرائتها . لعلها ذكرت في القرآن الكريم لهذا السبب . مثال على ذلك الآية التي تذكر أن النجوم موجودة لاستعمالها كالصواريخ ليضرب بها الشياطين

17 — هنالك آيات بتفاسير متضاربة . مثال على ذلك الآيات التي تذكر عن الخلق وإذا خلق الله الأرض مستديرة أو منبسطة . لقد ذكرت عدداً من هذه الآيات في هذا الكتاب . وحسب شرحها كما وردت في القرآن فهنالك لا مجال للشك أن الأرض خلقت منبسطة . هذه الآيات هي :

2/22
15/19
20/53
43/10
50/7

9 – لدي شعور بأن السجع والفقه الشعري في القرآن نال الإهتمام اكثر من الدقة اللغوية . ويجب أن أقر أنني استمتعت بذلك خلال قراءتي للقرآن .

10 – هناك آيات عديدة تتناقض مع الحقائق العلمية تماما وقد ذكرت بعضها سابقا ولا حاجة لإعادة ذكرها .

11 – إنه أكثر ما قرأت في حياتي تشويشا , فمثلا قصة النبي موسى متفرقة على مجموعة من السور فمن الصعب أن يقرأ المرء ضمن سورة واحدة , وكأن القصة قطعة معدنية مكونة من عدة أجزاء وكل جزء مخفي في مكان تحت الأرض وما عليك إلا أن تستعمل كاشفا معدنيا لجمع هذه القطع

12 – أنه أشد ما قرأت محيراً في حياتي . فمثلا هو يدعو إلى أمر ثم يعود فينصح بأمر آخر . مثلا هناك آيات تشير إلى عيسى (المسيح) كلمة الله وروح الله ,أنه تكلم في المهد صبيا وأنه خلق طير من الطين وشفى المجذوم وأقام الميت . فإذا كان الحال كذلك فإن عيسى هو الله وبذلك يكون مميزا عن الرسول النبي محمد . ولكن القرآن يشير إلى عيسى كأحد الرسل السابقين وهو أقل شأنا من النبي محمد (الذي وبالمناسبة لم يقم بأي عمل شابه المسيح بالرغم من توسل الناس إليه أن يقوم بمعجزة واحدة على الأقل)

13 – يبدو من الصعب أحيانا أن تحدد من الذي كتب القرآن فعلا , فبعض الآيات تبدأ هكذا " يطالبك الله أن تفعل هذا أو ذاك " بينما يجب أن تكون هكذا "أطلب منك (أنا) أن تفعل كذا وكذا " .يمكنني أن أخرج الكثير من الآيات ليرى القارىء أن كاتبها ليس الله . ولنأخذ هذه الآية كمثل : سورة آل عمران 3 آية 169 تنص " ولا تحسبن الذين قتلوا في سبيل الله أمواتا بل أحياء عند ربهم يرزقون " . فلو كان

4 – كثير من الآيات والسور (جمع سورة) تفتقد إلى العمق الروحي فمثلا سورة الفيل (105) :

آية – 1 – ألم تر كيف فعل ربك بأصحاب الفيل
آية – 2 – ألم يجعل كيدهم في تضليل
آية – 3 – وأرسل عليهم طيراً أبابيل
آية – 4 – ترميهم بحجارة من سجيل
آية – 5 – فجعلهم كعصف مأكول

هل يستطيع أحد أن يسأل نفسه بأمانة إن كان في هذه الآية أي محتوى روحاني . وهل هناك أي جدوى من إيرادها في القرآن

5 – هنالك عدد من الآيات بإشارة واضحة إلى الجنس وقد جاء تفصيلها خلال هذا الكتاب وليس هناك حاجة لإعادة ذكرها

6 – هنالك جمل وكلمات لا أرى مكانا لها في كتاب مقدس كالقرآن , مثل كلمة '' نكاح '' و ''فرج''

7 – هناك الكثير من المتناقضات , فبعض الآيات تدعو إلى السلام والمغفرة والرحمة وكذلك بعض الآيات تدعو إلى القتال والقتل وقطع الرؤوس والتعذيب ألخ .

8 – هنالك أخطاء إملائية و أخطاء لغوية أخرى . وهو المفروض أن يكون أهم ما كتب باللغة العربية , فمثلا كثيرا ما استعمل الفعل الماضي بدل المضارع وبالعكس , كما كتبت بعض الكلمات المنتهية بالتاء المقصورة بالتاء المفتوحة . وأنا متأكد أنه لو أراد أحد علماء اللغة لوجد الكثير من الأخطاء التي لا تبين لي .

الخاتمة

ملخص انطباعاتي من قراءتي للقرآن الكريم باختصار :

1 – يحتوي الكثير من التكرار . وكان بإمكان الله أن يختصره إلى النصف دون أن يتأثر محتواه , فمثلا سورة الكافرون (109) تنُص الآيات 2 و3 و4 و5 على نفس المعنى ولكن بكلمات مختلفة :
آية – 2 – لا أعبد ما تعبدون
آية – 3 – ولا أنتُم عابدون ما أعبد
آية – 4 – ولا أنا عابد ما عبدتم
آية – 5 – ولا أنتُم عابدون ما أعبد

2 – هنالك آيات ليس لها معنى مثل سورة التين (95) :
آية – 1 – والتين والزيتون
آية – 2 – وجبل سيناء
آية – 3 – وهذا البلد الأمين
ليس لهذه الآيات أي علاقة ببقية السورة

3 – هنالك آيات غامضة يصعب فهمها فمثلا سورة الإخلاص 112 الآية 2 تقول " الله الصمد"
لقد سألت صديقي ماذا تعني كلمة الصمد وقال أنه لا يعلم , ثم سألت وإياه بعض المصلين في المسجد وكانت إجاباتهم مختلفة حيث قال أحدهم أن معناها "المستقيم " وقال آخر أن معناها " المهيمن " وقال ثالث أن معناها " المثابر " . ومع هذا الإختلاف في التفسير قررنا أن نسأل ألإمام فأجاب أن معناها "الخالد " . فإذا كان هذا المعنى فلماذا لم يكن نص الآية "الخالد " أو " الأبدي " بلغة عربية بسيطة ومفهومة' . لذلك أنا لم أقتنع بكل هذه التفاسير ولا زلت لا أعرف معناها

111 – سورة المسد

1 – تبت يدا أبي لهب وتب

لماذا نتمنى الشر والضرر للآخرين في القرآن الكريم

3 – سيصلى ناراً ذات لهب

لماذا نتمنى الضرر لأي كان بدلا من نطلب له المغفرة من الله عن فعل أو قول أو أي ذنب آخر .

4- وامرأته حمالة الحطب

لماذا يعيب الله في القرآن على امرأة تحمل الحطب . أعتقد أن ذلك شديد الغرابة وما كان يجب أن يذكر شيء مثل هذا الأمر في القرآن الكريم عندما بحثت عن هذه السورة إكتشفت أن أبي لهب هو عم محمد ولكنه لم يؤمن برسالته وكان يستهزئ به أمام القوم فغضب الله على أبي لهب وأنزل هذه الآية في القرآن لتحقيره وامرأته طوال الزمن إني أرى أن تكون آية مثل هذه موجودة في القرآن في قمة العجب. كثيرا من الأنبياء أهينوا واحتقروا من قومهم ولكن الله لم يتدخل في أمور سخيفة مثل هذه لنشر دعوته . ليس من السهل نشر رسالة سماوية حيثما وأينما كان

79 - سورة النازعات

30 - والأرض بعد ذلك دحاها

مرة ثانية , الأرض مستديرة وليست منبسطة .

19 – ويطوف عليهم ولدان مخلدون إذا رأيتهم حسبتهم لؤلؤاً منثوراً

إن الطريقة التي يذكر فيها الأولاد تكاد تلمح إلى المشاعر الجنسية , فإذا كان الحال كذلك فإنه من العيب أن يجيء ذلك في نص القرآن الكريم . وأن يكون ذلك مسكوت عنه من قبل الله شديد القدسية وأكرم الأكرمين وأعظم المحبين .

20 – وإذا رأيت ثم رأيت نعيماً وملكاً كبيراً

أهذا توقعات لما عليه السماء ؟

21 – عاليهم ثياب سُندُس خُضر وإستبرق وحلوا أساور من فضة وسقاهم ربهم شراباً طهوراً

يا لله كل هذه الروعة في السماء , إضافة إلى أن يقوم الله بتقديم الشراب اللذيذ لنا ؟

76 - سورة الإنسان

12 - وجزاهم بما صبروا جنة وحريراً

جنة وحرير في السماء . من يعتني بالجنة ومن يغزل الحرير ؟

13 - متكئين فيها على الأرائك لا يرون فيها شمساً ولا زمهريراً

هذا ما نمارسه في هذا العالم !

14 - ودانية عليهم ظلالها وذللت قطوفها تذليلاً

جو شديد السكون , شبيه بـ وادي (نابا) في كاليفورنيا

15 - ويطاف عليهم بآنية من فضة وأكواب كانت قواريرا

غاية البذخ والدنيوية

16 - قواريرا من فضة قدروها تقديراً

أدوات نفيسة في السماء ؟؟

17 - ويُسقون فيها كأساً كان مزاجها زنجبيلاً

شراب لذيذ في السماء

18 - عيناً فيها تسمى سلسبيلاً

ينابيع طيبة في السماء

74 – سورة المدثر

31 – "كذلك يضل الله من يشاء ويهدي من يشاء"

هذه عبارة مشتقة من الآية (31). أود فقط أن أتساءل لماذا يفرق الله بين الناس كيفما يشاء. ألا ترون أن من الأفضل أن يتم التعامل مع الناس بالتساوي كل حسب أفعاله أو أفعالها. كثيرا ما يراودني شعور عندما أقرأ القرآن أن الله ليس عادلا. فالأولى أن يهدي الناس جميعا وليس فقط الذين يشاء منهم.

73 - سورة المزمل

20 - "يقاتلون في سبيل الله"

هذه عبارة مشتقة من الآية 20 ولكنني أحب أن أسأل لماذا يقوم الناس بالقتال من أجل الله . إن ذكر القتال والعنف يتكرر كثيرا في القرآن مع العلم أنه بملاك واحد من الملائكة يستطيع الله أن ينفذ جميع ما يطلب القرآن من الناس أن يقوموا به على الأرض . أتراني أجهل طبيعة الله وقدرته الفائقة في تحقيق ما يريد , فلماذا يطلب الله منا أن نقاتل ونقطع الرؤوس ونذبح ونعذب الآخرين بالنيابة عنه .

71 - سورة نوح

15 – ألم تروا كيف خلق الله سبع سماوات طباقاً

ها نحن نعود إلى السماء ذات السبع طبقات . هل يقوم أحد الناس بالنظر في الأمر للتأكد إن كان هذا الكلام حقيقيا أم أنه من نسج الخيال ,لأنني لست مختصا علميا

19 – والله جعل لكم الأرض بساطاً

آية أخرى بما معناه أن الأرض منبسطة وليست مستديرة

70 - سورة المعارج

29 - والذين هم لفروجهم حافظون

هل هذا نص يليق بالقرآن الكريم ؟ألم يكن بالإمكان إستعمال نص آخر كأن يقال " يحافظ على عفتهن " ولا شك أن في اللغة العربية ألفاظا مشابهة كثيرة , ولكنني لا أستطيع أن أستوعب لماذا ترد في القرآن ألفاظ جارحة في عدة مناسبات , وكأن الله مهتم بما هو جنس أو أنه عاجز عن اختيار أنسب الكلمات في اللغة العربية

30 – إلا على أزواجهم أو ما ملكت أيمانهم فإنهم غير ملومين

هذه الآية تكملة للآية 29 وتعني أن النساء يجب أن لا يمارسن الجنس إلا مع أزواجهن ولكن أزواجهن يسمح لهم ممارسة الجنس مع ما ملكت أيمانهم أيضا أليس هذا تحقيرا لمن ملكت أيمانهم أن يكونوا للهو الرجال حيثما وأينما أرادوا ؟!

67 – سورة الملك

3 – الذي خلق سبع سماوات طباقاً ما ترى في خلق الرحمن من تفاوت فارجع البصر هل ترى من فطور

لم أسمع عن سبع سماوات واحدة فوق الأخرى . هل ثبت ذلك علميا ؟ قد أكون جاهلا بهذه الأمور العلمية لكونها خارج تخصصي العلمي . ولذلك قد يكون القرآن يخبر عن أمور لم يتم اكتشافها بعد . ولكن ألا تقول الآية "فارجع البصر هل ترى من فطور " ؟ وهذا يعني يمكننا أن نراها ؟؟؟!!!

5 – ولقد زينا السماء الدنيا بمصابيح وجعلناها رجوما للشياطين واعتدنا لهم عذاب السعير

أليس من الغريب أن تصور هذه النجوم التي نرى في السماء كصواريخ لضرب الشياطين . المفهوم أن هناك عددا كبيرا من النجوم . فما على المرء إلا أن ينظر إلى السماء في ليل صاف ويحاول أن يعد النجوم في القاطع الذي يستطيع أن يراه حيث يكون , فقد يقضي عمره كاملا وهو يقوم بالعد . هل يعني ذلك أن هنالك هذا العدد من الشياطين أو أن كل شيطان يحتاج إلى عدد كبير من النجوم للقضاء عليه ؟ هل يستطيع أحد أن يفسر هذه الظاهرة المحيرة .؟؟؟!!!

66 - سورة التحريم

9 - يأيها النبي جاهد الكفار والمنافقين واغلظ عليهم ومأواهم جهنم وبئس المصير

أليس من الأفضل مخاطبة الكفار والمنافقين بالحسنى فلعلهم يقتنعون بالإيمان الصحيح

12 - ومريم ابنت عمران التى أحصنت فرجها فنفخنا فيه من روحنا وصدقت بكلمات ربها وكتبه وكانت من القانتين

لا أكاد أصدق أن هذا النص في القرآن . كما لا أصدق أن ينفخ الله روحه في فرج مريم . ألم يكن من الممكن لله القادر على كل شيء أن يختار جزء آخر من جسدها أو ينفخ روحه فيها عن بعد بدلا من أن يختار الفرج عن أي جزء آخر لقد علمتني قرائتي في اللغة العربية أن كلمة "إبنت" يجب أن تنتهي بحرف "ة" المربوطة هكذا "إبنة"، وليس بحرف "ت" المفتوحة كما وردت في القرآن . هذا يعني أن الله الذي لا يخطىء وخاصة باللغة العربية قد أخطأ في الإملاء وكان على شخص مثلي (لا يمت للعرب بأي صلة) أن يصححه .

65 – سورة الطلاق

4 – واللائي يئسن من المحيض من نسائكم إن ارتبتم فعدتهن ثلاثة أشهر واللائي لم يحضن وأولات الأحمال أجلهن أن يضعن حملهن ومن يتق الله يجعل له من أمره يسراً

أقرأ هذه الآية وأنا في غاية الانزعاج. لا أدر كيف يسمح الله بممارسة الجنس مع القاصرات قبل أن يحضن

12—الله الذي خلق سبع سماوات ومن الأرض مثلهن يتنزل الأمر بينهن لتعلموا أن الله على كل شيء قدير وأن الله قد أحاط بكل شيء علما

هذه أول مرة أعرف أن هناك سبع سماوات ومثلها سبع أرضين. لقد وصل علم الفضاء إلى مرحلة متقدمة جدا في علم الفضاء حيث أنه بإمكاننا رؤية مجرات ملايين السنين الضوئية بعيدة عنا في عمق الفضاء والتي ندعوها السماء , وحتى الآن لم نرى إلا سماء واحدة وأرض واحدة . فدعك من سماء أو أرض ثانية وثالثة ورابعة وخامسة وسادسة وسابعة . بالنسبة لي أعتبر كل هذا هراء عاري من الصحة ماما .

62 - سورة الجمعة

5- مثل الذين حملوا التوراة ثم لم يحملوها كمثل الحمار يحمل أسفارا بئس مثل القوم الذين كذبوا بآيات الله والله لا يهدى القوم الظالمين

ما هذا التفكير بالناس وتشبيههم بالحمير ؟! هل تحب نفس هؤلاء الناس أن ينعتوك بالحمار لأنك لا تأخذ بتعاليمهم

61 – سورة الصف

4 – إن الله يحب الذين يقاتلون في سبيله صفاً كأنهم بنيان مرصوص

إن الله يحب الذين يقاتلون من أجله ؟؟؟

60 – سورة الممتحنة

1 – يأيها الذين آمنوا لا تتخذوا عدوي وعدوكم أولياء تلقون إليهم بالمودة وقد كفروا بما جاءكم من الحق يخرجون الرسول وإياكم أن تؤمنوا بالله ربكم إن كنتم خرجتم جهاداً في سبيلي وابتغاء مرضاتي تسرون إليهم بالمودة وأنا أعلم بما أخفيتم وما أعلنتم ومن يفعله منكم فقد ضل سواء السبيل

تبين هذه الآية أن الله متعصب لا يقبل أي مخالف .

10 – يأيها الذين آمنوا إذا جاءكم المؤمنات مهاجرات فامتحنوهن الله أعلم بإيمانهن فإن علمتموهن مؤمنات فلا ترجعوهن إلى الكفار لا هن حل لهم ولا هم يحلون لهن وآتوهم ما أنفقوا ولا جناح عليكم أن تنكحوهن إذا آتيتموهن أجورهن ولا تمسكوا بعصم الكوافر واسألوا ما أنفقتم وليسألوا ما أنفقوا ذلكم حكم الله يحكم بينكم والله عليم حكيم

أليس من العجيب أن يسمح الله بممارسة الجنس مقابل المال ؟

59 – سورة الحشر

23 – هو الله الذى لا إله إلا هو الملك القدوس السلام المؤمن المهيمن العزيز الجبار المتكبر سبحان الله عما يشركون

أعتقد أن وصف الله بالمتكبر وصف غير مقبول . وكذلك وصف الله بالمؤمن . ''المؤمن'' بماذا ؟

58 – سورة المجادلة

22 - لا تجد قوما يؤمنون بالله واليوم الآخر يوادون من حاد الله ورسوله ولو كانوا آباءهم أو ابناءهم أو إخوانهم أو عشيرتهم أولئك كتب فى قلوبهم الإيمان وأيدهم بروح منه ويدخلهم جنات تجري من تحتها الأنهار خالدين فيها رضي الله عنهم ورضوا عنه أولئك حزب الله ألا إن حزب الله هم المفلحون

إن هذه الآية القرآنية مبهمه وغير معقولة وغير أخلاقية حيث تحث على التفرقة بين أفراد الأسرة الواحدة . كيف يتوقع الله مني أن أكون ضد عائلتي لأنهم يعتقدون غير ما أعتقد ؟ ليحاسبهم الله بعد الموت كما يشاء . لماذا يثير الكراهية بيني وبين أهلي ؟ هذا بينما تنص الآية 6 من سورة الكافرون '' لكم دينكم ولي دين'' ما هذا التناقض الغريب . أعتقد أن الله يريدنا أن نحب بعضنا بعضا وليس أن نكره بعضنا بعضا إذا هو الله العادل المحب

57 – سورة الحديد

10 – وما لكم ألا تنفقوا في سبيل الله ولله ميراث السماوات والأرض لا يستوى منكم من أنفق من قبل الفتح وقاتل أولئك أعظم درجة من الذين أنفقوا من بعد وقاتلوا وكلا وعد الله الحسنى والله بما تعملون خبير

وهنا يكافئ الله الذين بادروا قبل غيرهم بالقتال أكثر من الذين التحقوا بالقتال متأخرين. وماذا عن الذين لم يسمعوا ما الذي يريده الله إلا بعد حين ؟

22 – وحور عين

هل النساء للمعاشرة الجنسية ؟ ما هي مهمتهن ؟!

23- كأمثال اللؤلؤ المكنون

ما هي الصفات الخاصة باللؤلؤ ؟

28 –في سدر مخضود

هل هذا في الجنة ؟

29 – وطلح منضود

وهذا أيضا في السماء ؟

30 – وظل ممدود

وهل تتألق الشمس هناك أيضا ؟

31 – وماء مسكوب

وهل يعطشون في السماء ؟ -

32 – وفاكهة كثيرة

يبدو أن الفواكه في الجنة لا تنقطع .

34 – وفرش مرفوعة

وهل ينامون في الجنة ؟ هل ترى يوجد ليل ونهار في الجنة وهل ينامون قيلولة بعد الظهر ؟ يبدو أنه يوجد أشياء كثيرة في السماء ونحن نجهلها

36 – فجعلناهن أبكاراً

ما هي الحاجة إلى العذارى في السماء ؟ ولماذا يشغل الله نفسه في هذه الأمور المبتذلة في القرآن الكريم؟!

56 - سورة الواقعة

15 - على سرر موضونة
هل يعقل أن يكون ذلك في الجنة ؟

16 - متكئين عليها متقابلين
ماذا يعني هذا ؟ هل المقصود تأمين حالة استرخاء مطلقة

17 - يطوف عليهم ولدان مخلدون
مرة ثانية يذكر الأولاد , لماذا لا يذكر الملائكة ؟

18 - بأكواب وأباريق وكأس من معين
هل هذا احتفال مع الخدم ؟

20- وفاكهة مما يتخيرون
هل تتوفر جميع أنواع الفاكهة في السماء ؟!

21 - ولحم طير مما يشتهون
هل يأكلونها نيئة ؟ أو من يقوم بالطبخ ؟ هل هم الأولاد أيضا أم الملائكة أو الرجال أنفسهم أو أن هناك طباخون جهزهم الله لهذا الغرض . وهل هنالك مطبخ وإذا كان كذلك فمن يغسل الصحون والقدور ؟

52 – سورة الطور

20 – متكئين على سرر مصفوفة وزوجناهم بحور عين

مرة أخرى أراني مستغربا لأمر الزواج في الجنة ؟!

22 – وأمددناهم بفاكهة ولحم مما يشتهون

انهم يأكلون ويشربون في الجنة ولا يوجد ذكر للعرق والبول والخرائة . هل ترى يوجد مراحيض وحمامات وغير ذلك ؟!

23 – يتنازعون فيها كأسا لا لغو فيها ولا تأثيم

وهناك كؤوس مملوءة مشروبات

24 - ويطوف عليهم غلمان لهم كأنهم لؤلؤ مكنون

لماذا يذكر ''الأولاد'' وليس الملائكة ، إن ذلك يدعو إلى الحيرة , فهل المقصود الإيحاء بالتحرش بالأولاد .

51 - سورة الذاريات

48 – والأرض فرشناها فنعم الماهدون

الأرض مستديرة وليست منبسطة

49 - ومن كل شيء خلقنا زوجين لعلكم تذكرون

هذا ليس صحيحاً البتة , فقد تعلمتُ في مدرستي الثانوية أن هناك مخلوقات خنثى , أي أنها تحتوي على أعضاء تناسلية ذكرية وأنثوية في آن واحد . أيضا هناك مخلوقات لا يوجد فيها أعضاء تناسلية إطلاقا ولكنها تنقسم تلقائيا إلى إثنين والإثنين إلى أربعة وهلم جرى وهكذا تتكاثر . هذا يعني أنه لا حاجة دائما لزوجين للتكاثر

50 - سورة ق

7 - والأرض مددناها وألقينا فيها رواسي وأنبتنا فيها من كل زوج بهيج

مرة أخرى ألأرض مستديرة وليست مبسطة.

49 - سورة الحجرات

9 - وإن طائفتان من المؤمنين اقتتلوا فأصلحوا بينهما فإن بغت إحداهما على الأخرى فقاتلوا التي تبغي حتى تفيء الى أمر الله فإن فاءت فأصلحوا بينهما بالعدل وأقسطوا إن الله يحب المقسطين

لماذا المبادرة إلى قتال المعتدي بدلاً عن البحث عن وسيلة سلمية أخرى . انه من الغريب أنه على مدى القرآن يبدو أن اللجوء إلى العنف هو في مقدمة الخيارات

48 – سورة الفتح

9 – لتؤمنوا بالله ورسوله، وتعزروه وتوقروه وتسبحوه بُكرةً وأصيلاً

لماذا كل هذا التعظيم للرسول , وما هو إلا حامل لرسالة من الله , وهو إنسان مثلنا

14 – ولله ملك السماوات والأرض يغفر لمن يشاء ويعذب من يشاء، وكان الله غفوراً رحيماً

لماذا يغفر الله لمن يشاء ويعاقب من يشاء ؟ وإذا الله كان غفوراً رحيماً فهل لا يزال كذلك ؟

16- قل للمخلفين من الأعراب ستدعون إلى قوم أولى بأس شديد تقاتلونهم أو يسلمون فإن تطيعوا يؤتكم الله أجراً حسناً وإن تتولوا كما توليتم من قبلُ يعذبكم عذاباً أليماً

الله يعذب القوم الذين لا يقاتلون في سبيله ؟!

47 – سورة محمد

4 – فإذا لقيتم الذين كفروا فضرب الرقاب حتى إذا أثخنتموهم فشدوا الوثاق فإما منا بعد وإما فداء حتى تضع الحرب أوزارها ذلك ولو يشاء الله لانتصر منهم ولكن ليبلو بعضكم ببعض والذين قتلوا فى سبيل الله فلن يضل أعمالهم

لماذا هذا القتال المتواصل على الكفرة , ولماذا هذا الحث على العنف من الله ؟

15 – مثل الجنة التى وعد المتقون فيها أنهار من ماء غير أسن وأنهار من لبن لم يتغير طعمه ، وأنهار من خمر لذة للشاربين وأنهار من عسل مصفى ولهم فيها من كل الثمرات ومغفرة من ربهم كمن هو خالد في النار وسقوا ماءً حميماً فقطع أمعاءهم

إنها لجنة خيالية بالمقارنة إلى جهنم ؟

35 – فلا تهنوا وتدعوا إلى السلم وأنتم الأعلون والله معكم ولن يتركم أعمالكم

أليس من الأفضل أن يسعى إلى السلام وهو في موقع القوة لكي يتلافى المزيد من العنف , ولكن يبدو أن الله ليس متسامحا ولكنه يحب أن يذل الناس بالعنف

44 - سورة الدخان

52 - في جنات وعيون
يوجد في عالمنا حدائق وينابيع , فهل تلك التي في السماء مختلفة ؟

53 - يلبسون من سندس واستبرق متقابلين
وكأنهم يستعدون للذهاب إلى احتفال كبير ؟!

54 - كذلك وزوجناهم بحور عين
لم يخطر ببالي أن الأرواح تتزاوج في الآخرة , وبالمناسبة هل ستتزوج النساء من رجال بيض العيون ؟

55 - يدعون فيها بكل فاكهة آمنين
ما أجمل أن تتوفر للمرء الفواكه بشكل دائم في السماء

43 - سورة الزخرف

3 – إنا جعلناه قرءاناً عربياً لعلكم تعقلون

لماذا يكون القرآن باللغة العربية فقط . وماذا عن الذين لا يعرفون اللغة العربية

10 – الذى جعل لكم الأرض مهداً وجعل لكم فيها سبلاً لعلكم تهتدون

كل ما أعرفه علمياً أن الأرض مستديرة وليست منبسطة

71 – يطاف عليهم بصحاف من ذهب وأكواب وفيها ما تشتهيه الأنفس وتلذ الأعين وأنتم فيها خالدون

لم يخطر لي أن هذه الأشياء موجودة في السماء ؟

72 – وتلك الجنة التي أورثتموها بما كنتم تعملون

أنها جنة دنيوية ولكنها خالدة

73 – لكم فيها فاكهة كثيرة منها تأكلون

هل تختلف هذه الفواكه عن الفواكه الموجودة في عالمنا ؟ مجرد خاطرة

52 - وكذلك أوحينا إليك روحاً من أمرنا ، ما كنت تدري ما الكتاب ولا الإيمان ولكن جعلناه نوراً نهدي به من نشاء من عبادنا وإنك لتهدى إلى صراط مستقيم

لماذا يهدي الله من يشاء ولا يهدي جميع الناس

42 – سورة الشورى

8 – ولو شاء الله لجعلهم أمةً واحدةً ولكن يدخل من يشاء في رحمته ، والظالمون ما لهم من ولى ولا نصير

إن الله يميز بعض الناس عن غيرهم

13 – شرع لكم من الدين ما وصى به نوحاً والذى أوحينا إليك وما وصينا به إبراهيم وموسى وعيسى أن أقيموا الدين ولا تتفرقوا فيه كبر على المشركين ما تدعوهم إليه ، الله يجتبي إليه من يشاء ويهدي إليه من ينيب

كنت أعتقد أن الله يجذب نحوه جميع الناس

19 – الله لطيف بعباده ، يرزق من يشاء ، وهو القوي العزيز

لماذا يعطي الله بعض الناس وليس كل الناس

50 – او يزوجهم ذكرانا وإناثا ويجعل من يشاء عقيماً ، إنه عليم قدير

لماذا يختار الله أن يجعل بعض الناس عاجزين عن الإنجاب ؟ أليس في ذلك ظلم

41 - سورة فصلت

3 – كتاب فصلت آياته قرءاناً عربياً لقوم يعلمون

وماذا عن الناس الذين لا يفهمون ولا يعرفون اللغة العربية

12 – فقضاهن سبع سماوات في يومين وأوحى في كل سماء أمرها وزينا السماء الدنيا بمصابيح وحفظاً ذلك تقدير العزيز العليم

الذي أعرفه أن هناك سماء واحدة , إلا إذا أثبت علميا غير ذلك

73- وسيق الذين اتقوا ربهم الى الجنة زُمراً حتى إذا جاءوها وفتحت أبوابها وقال لهم خزنتها سلام عليكم طبتم فادخلوها خالدين

أليس من الغريب أن يكون في الجنة حدائق لها بوابات وبوابون . هل حتى في السماء هناك خوف من قطاع طرق ويجب الحماية والخوف منهم ؟!

39 - سورة الزمر

20 - لكن الذين اتقوا ربهم لهم غرف من فوقها غرف مبنية تجرى من تحتها الأنهار وعد الله لايخلف الله الميعاد

ما كنت أظن أن في الجنة بنايات متعددة الطبقات وأنهارا جارية , وهل هذه المباني مشيدة من الطابوق والإسمنت والحديد أو من مواد سماوية لا نعلمها

28 - قرءاناً عربياً غير ذي عوج لعلهم يتقون

لماذا يجب أن يكون القرآن باللغة العربية وليس بلغات أخرى ليهتدي الآخرون . أليس ذلك تحيزا ؟

52 - أولم يعلموا أن الله يبسط الرزق لمن يشاء ويقدر ، إن في ذلك لآيات لقوم يؤمنون

لماذا يكون لله نظرة تفضيلية لبعض الناس عن بعضهم الآخر ؟!

60 - ويوم القيامة ترى الذين كذبوا على الله وجوههم مسودة ، أليس في جهنم مثوى للمتكبرين

أليس في ذلك عنصرية ضد السود , من الأفضل أن يقال إبيضت وجوههم فمن المعلوم أنه عندما يخاف الناس تبيض وجوههم . لقد ذكر ألله اللون الأسود متعمدا لتحقير من في جهنم

37 - سورة الصافات

125 - أتدعون بعلاً وتذرون أحسن الخالقين

هل تعني هذه الآية أن هناك أكثر من خالق واحد ولكن ״الله القرآني״ أفضلهم ؟!

36 – سورة يس

38 – والشمس تجري لمستقر لها ، ذلك تقدير العزيز العليم

العلم يفيد بأن الشمس لا تتحرك . (حتى إذا تفسير ما جاء في القرآن على أن حركة الشمس هي جزء من حركة المجرة فإنه لا يوجد لها مكان تغيب فيه)

56 – هم وأزواجهم في ظلال على الأرائك متكئون

هذا يعطي الانطباع بأن الناس يتزوجون في الجنة وأن هناك شمس ودرجة حرارة مرتفعة بحيث يجد الناس أنفسهم بحالة كسل ليستلقوا على أرائكهم في الظل

57 – لهم فيها فاكهة ولهم ما يدعون

تبدو جنة عدن في القرآن كأنها كرم فواكه حقيقي

35 - سورة فاطر

8 - أفمن زُين له سوء عمله فرآه حسناً فإن الله يضل من يشاء ويهدى من يشاء فلا تذهب نفسك عليهم حسرات ، إن الله عليم بما يصنعون

لماذا يقوم الإله المحب بتضليل بعض الناس

33 - جنات عدن يدخلونها يحلون فيها من أساور من ذهب ولؤلؤاً ولباسهم فيها حرير

لم أكن أفكر بأن في جنة عدن مثل هذه الأشياء الدنيوية

34 – سورة سبأ

36 – قل إن ربى يبسط الرزق لمن يشاء ويقدر ولكن أكثر الناس لا يعلمون

لماذا لا يكون عطاء الله متساوياً للجميع

39 – قل إن ربى يبسط الرزق لمن يشاء من عباده ويقدر له، وما أنفقتم من شيء فهو يخلفه ، وهو خير الرازقين

مرة أخرى لا يكون عطاء الله متساويا , لماذا يفضل البعض على غيرهم

61 – ملعونين أينما ثُقفوا أُخذوا وقُتلوا تقتيلاً

بحق السماء لماذا كل هذا العنف في القرآن الكريم

64 – إن الله لعن الكافرين وأعد لهم سعيراً

لماذا تبدو كراهية الله في القرآن بهذه القسوة ,
بينما تنص آيات أخرى على أن الله شديد الرحمة
والغفران . إن ذلك في غاية التناقض

50- يأيها النبي إنا أحللنا لك أزواجك اللاتي أتيت أجورهن وما ملكت يمينك مما أفاء الله عليك وبنات عمك وبنات عماتك وبنات خالك وبنات خالاتك اللاتي هاجرن معك وإمرأة مؤمنة إن وهبت نفسها للنبي إن أراد النبي أن يستنكحها خالصة لك من دون المؤمنين ، قد علمنا ما فرضنا عليهم في أزواجهم وما ملكت أيمانهم لكيلا يكون عليك حرج وكان الله غفوراً رحيماً

كأنما الله يقدم خدمات جنسية للنبي ولكن ليس لغيره من المؤمنين , ثم لماذا استعمال الفعل الماضي لغفر الله ورحمته بدلا من استعمال الفعل المضارع . كأن يقال إن الله غفور رحيم

51 – ترجى من تشاء منهن وتؤوي إليك من تشاء ومن ابتغيت ممن عزلت فلا جناح عليك ذلك أدنى أن تقر أعينهن ولا يحزن ويرضين بما أتيتهن كلهن والله يعلم ما في قلوبكم وكان الله عليماً حليماً

يلاحظ المزيد من محاباة الله للنبي

56 – إن الله وملائكته يصلون على النبي ، يأيها الذين آمنوا صلوا عليه وسلموا تسليماً

ما كنت أعلم أن الله يصلي للنبي , أليس ذلك مستغربا ؟!

57 – إن الذين يؤذون الله ورسوله لعنهم الله في الدنيا والآخرة وأعد لهم عذاباً مهيناً

لماذا يقوم الله بتجهيز وسائل التعذيب لمن يسيئون للنبي , وماذا لو تابوا لاحقا ؟

37 - وإذ تقول للذي أنعم الله عليه وأنعمت عليه أمسك عليك زوجك واتق الله وتخفي في نفسك ما الله مبديه وتخشى الناس والله أحق أن تخشاه فلما قضى زيد منها وطراً زوجناكها لكي لا يكون على المؤمنين حرج في أزواج أدعيائهم إذا قضوا منهن وطراً وكان أمر الله مفعولاً

حاشا لله أن يسمح للرجال بالزواج من زوجات أبنائهم بالتبني

40 - ما كان محمد أبا أحد من رجالكم ولكن رسول الله وخاتم النبيين وكان الله بكل شيء عليماً

هناك رجال أدعوا النبوة بعد محمد ولهم أتباع كثيرون . فهناك مثلا " جوزف سميث" في الولايات المتحدة والحركة "المرمونية" , وهناك"ميرزا غلام أحمد" من مواليد الهند وقد إدعى أنه المسيح المنتظر وهناك حركة "داهش بيه" التي بدأت في فلسطين ثم امتدت إلى لبنان ومنها إلى الولايات المتحدة حيث توفي وله متحف وعدة كتب باسمه . وله صلاة مثل الفاتحة عند المسلمين والصلاة الربانية عند المسيحيين . وهناك " بهاء الدين " الذي ابتدا في إيران وله الحركة البهائية وتوفي في إسرائيل . أذن محمد ليس خاتم الأنبياء . ومرة أخرى يستعمل الفعل الماضي , لماذا لا يقول الله يعلم كل شيء

33 - سورة الأحزاب

1 - ياأيها النبي اتق الله ولا تطع الكافرين والمنافقين ، إن الله كان عليماً حكيماً

إذا كان القرآن كلمة الله , فلماذا يستعمل الله صيغة الفعل الماضي بالنسبة للمعرفة والحكمة . حيث يجب أن يكون النص إن الله عليم حكيم . مرة ثانية هذا يعني أن الله ليس ضليعا باللغة العربية . وهو الآن ليس ''عليماً حكيماً''،

26 - وأنزل الذين ظاهروهم من أهل الكتاب من صياصيهم وقذف في قلوبهم الرعب ، فريقاً تقتلون وتأسرون فريقا

لماذا ينشد الله العنف

27 وأورثكم أرضهم وديارهم وأموالهم وأرضاً لم تطئوها وكان الله على كل شيء قديراً

الله يؤيد السلب وهذا أمر غريب

32 – سورة السجدة

4 – اللهُ الذي خلق السماوات والأرض وما بينهما في ستة أيام ثم استوى على العرش ما لكم من دونه من ولي ولا شفيع أفلا تتذكرون

نعود ثانية لذكر العرش , أي عرش هذا ؟

13 – ولو شئنا لأتينا كل نفس هداها ولكن حق القول مني لأملأن جهنم من الجنة والناس أجمعين

علمنا أن الله غفور رحيم وها هو يريد أن يملأ جهنم من الناس والجن

31 – سورة لقمان

19 – واقصد في مشيك واغضُض من صوتك إن أنكر الأصوات لصوت الحمير

كيف يأتي هذا القول من قبل الله , ولماذا يعتبر صوت الحمير هو الأسوأ في حين أن هناك بين الناس من يعجبه صوت نهيق الحمير

29 – سورة العنكبوت

21 – يعذب من يشاء ويرحم من يشاء وإليه تُقلبون

يبدو من ذلك أن قدرنا محدد مسبقا , وإذا كان ذلك فإن الله ليس عادلا

62 – الله يبسط الرزق لمن يشاء من عباده ويقدرُ له ، إن الله بكل شيء عليم

كيف يفضل الله بعض الناس على غيرهم . أين العدل ؟

64 – وما هذه الحياة الدنيا إلا لهو ولعب وإن الدار الأخرة لهي الحيوان لو كانوا يعلمون

ماذا تعني هذه الآية ؟ أعتقد أكثر إحتمال أنها تعني حياة بدون مسئولية كالحيوانات . ولكن حينما استفسرت عن المعنى لكلمة الحيوان في هذه الآية قيل لي أن المعنى هنا "الحياة" . إذا كان هذا المعنى, فلماذا لم يذكر الله ذلك لكي لا تكون الآية غامضة وبحاجة إلى استفسار لفهمها . هل كان الله يريد تعقيد الأمور لفهم رسالته ؟

28 – اذهب بكتابي هذا فالقه إليهم ثم تولَّ عنهم فانظر ماذا يرجعون

لقد أثبت الهدهد أنه أفضل جاسوس عرفه العالم من غير البشر

39 – قال عفريت من الجن أنا أتيك به قبل أن تقوم من مقامك ,وإني عليه لقوي أمين

هنا الجن يطمئنون الملك سليمان أنه قادر على هزيمة سبأ . وإني لأتساءل إن كان أحد قد حاول أن يفهم الفائدة الروحية من ورود قصة الملك سليمان والنمل الناطق والهدهد الذكي في القرآن الكريم ؟ لا بد أن يكون لهذا النص معنى يعجز العقل البشري عن فهمه وإلا لما كان لها أن تذكر في أحد أهم الإيحات الموجهة للبشرية . كما أنه يخطر لي أن أتساءل ماذا كانت ستكون النتيجة لو تم سحق النمل تحت أقدام الجيش أو أن كان الهدهد قد استبدل برسول بشري ؟! . هل ستكون النتيجة نفسها ؟ .

22 – فمكثَ غير بعيد فقال أحطتُ بما لم
تُحط به وجئتك من سبأ بنبأ يقين

هل يستطيع الهدهد أيضا أن يتكلم ويعطي معلومات مهمة

23 – أني وجدت امرأة تملكهم وأوتيت
من كل شيء ولها عرش عظيم

عجيب أمر هذا الهدهد

24 – وجدتها وقومها يسجدون للشمس من دون الله وزين
لهم الشيطان أعمالهم فصدهم عن السبيل فهم لا يهتدون

يا لنباهة هذا الهدهد , فلا شك أنه كان جاسوسا قديرا

25 – ألا يسجدوا لله الذي يُخرجُ الخبءَ في
السماوات والأرض ويعلم ما تخفون وما تعلنون

يا للعجب , إنه هدهد مفكر وحكيم

26 – ألله لا إله إلا هو ربُّ العرش العظيم

ها هو الهدهد يشهد بأن الله واحد . كم هو عظيم هذا الهدهد

27 – قال سننظر أصدقت أم كنت من الكاذبين

هل من العدالة أن يشك الملك سليمان بأقوال
جاسوسه الهدهد , بعد كل ما عمله هذا من
مخاطرة خلال تنفيذ عمله كجاسوس

27 – سورة النمل

17 – وحُشر لسليمان جنوده من الجن والأنس والطير فهم يوزعون

لأول مرة أسمع بجيش من الجن والطيور

18 – وحتى إذا أتوا على وادي النمل قالت نملة يا ايها النمل أدخلوا مساكنكم لا يحطمنكم سليمان وجنوده وهم لا يشعرون

أليس من المستغرب أن ينطق النمل لكي يتجنب الإبادة

19 – فتبسم ضاحكاً من قولها وقال رب أوزعني أن أشكر نعمتك التي أنعمت علي وعلى والديَّ وأن أعمل صالحا ترضاه وأدخلني برحمتك في عبادك الصالحين

أليس من الغريب أن يفهم سليمان لغة النمل ؟ هذا إذا كان للنمل لغة , فإنني ومعظم الناس لم نسمع بها أبدا

20 – وتفقد الطير فقال مالي لا أرى الهدهد أم كان من الغائبين

وهل يحتاج الهدهد إلى إذن للغياب

21 – لأعذبنه عذاباً شديداً أو لأذبحنه أو ليأتيني بسلطان مبين

أهذا ما يتوقعه المرء من ملك وطير

26 – سورة الشعراء

195 – بلسان عربى مبين
لماذا يكون باللغة العربية فقط

25 - سورة الفرقان

59 – الذى خلق السماوات والأرض وما بينهما في ستة أيام ثم استوى على العرش الرحمن ، فاسأل به خبيراً

ماذا تعني العرش الرحمان , ومن له الخبرة لكي يعرف إذا هذا صحيحا أم لا . قيل لي المعنى هنا أن الرحمان استوى على العرش . إذا كان هذا صحيحا فهذا يعني أن الله لا يتقن اللغة العربية كما يدعى . كيف لي وأنا لا أمت للعرب بأي شكل كان أن أتقن اللغة العربية أحسن من إله القرآن. لأنني لو أردت أن أكتب هذه الآية سأكتبها على الشكل التالي:
"الذي خلق السماوات والأرض وما بينهما في ستة أيام ثم استوى الرحمن على العرش , فاسأل به خبيراً "

24 – سورة النور

2 – الزانية والزاني فاجلدوا كل واحد منهما مائة جلدة ولا تأخذكم بهما رأفة في دين الله إن كنتم تؤمنون بالله واليوم الآخر وليشهد عذابهما طائفة من المؤمنين

لماذا يُعير ويُعاقب من يرتكب الزنى وإن بموافقة الطرفين , بينما يتغاضى الله عندما يمارس المرء الجنس مع سباياه وإن كان ذلك يجري بما يشبه الإغتصاب .

23 - سورة المؤمنون

5 - والذين هم لفروجهم حافظون

أي نطق مثل هذا يرد في القرآن ؟ ألم يكن ممكناً أن يقال مثلا "النساء اللاتي يتجنبن العلاقات الجنسية مع الرجال "

6 - إلا على أزواجهم أو ما ملكت أيمانهم فإنهم غير ملومين

لماذا لا يلام من يستغل المستعبدات , أذلك لأنهن عاجزات عن المقاومة

14 - ثم خلقنا النطفة علقة فخلقنا العلقة مضغة فخلقنا المضغة عظاماً فكسونا العظام لحماً ثم أنشأناه خلقاً آخر فتبارك الله أحسن الخالقين

إن هذه الآية تناقض كل ما جاء في علم الأحياء الذي يقول أن البيضة الملقحة (وهي مركبة من السائل المنوي والبويضة) تتحول إلى كتلة من الخلايا التي تدخل في سلسلة من التطورات وتتشعب إلى أعضاء مختلفة من الجسم ومنها الغضروف ثم إلى العظام . وعليه , فلا يوجد هناك دم ولا عظام تكتسي لاحقاً باللحم . إضافة إلى ذلك . أن يقال أن الله أفضل الخالقين ,وكأنك تقول أن هناك كثيراً من الخالقين وان الله أعظمهم .

86 - قل من ربُّ السماوات السبع ورب العرش العظيم

أي سبع سماوات وأي عرش عظيم

22 – سورة الحج

16 – وكذلك أنزلناهُ آيات بينات وأنَ الله يهدي من يُريدُ

إذا كان الله يهدي من يشاء , فما هو دوري كمؤمن ؟

65 – ألم ترَ أن الله سخر لكم ما في الأرض والفلك تجري في البحر بأمره ويمسك السماء أن تقع على الأرض إلا بإذنه ، إن الله بالناس لرءوف رحيم

كيف يقوم الله بالإمساك بالسماء لكي لا تقع على الأرض ؟

21 – سورة الأنبياء

30 – أوَلم يرَ الذين كفروا أن السماوات والأرض كانتا رتقاً ففتقناهما وجعلنا من الماء كل شيء حي أفلا يؤمنون

لا يمكنني أن أحقق في هذه الآية لأنها تعالج موضوع خلق السماوات والأرض. وفي أي حال لست مقتنعاً بها. زائد على ذلك هذه أول مرة أعلم أن كل الكائنات الحية معمولة من الماء. لو ذكر أن الماء شيء أساسي للحياة سيكون لذلك وقع أكبر.

20 – سورة طه

5 – الرحمان على العرش استوى

أي عرش هذا ؟ إن العروش للملوك والأباطرة

53 - الذى جعل لكم الأرض مهداً وسلك لكم فيها سبلاً وأنزل من السماء ماءً فأخرجنا به أزواجاً من نبات شتى

الأرض مستديرة وليست منبسطة

113 – وكذلك أنزلناه قرآنا عربياً وصرفنا فيه من الوعيد لعلهم يتقون او يُحدثُ لهم ذكراً

وماذا بشأن الناس الذين لا يعرفون اللغة العربية

18 - سورة الكهف

86 – حتى إذا بلغ مغرب الشمس وجدها تغرب فى عين حمئة ووجد عندها قوماً قلنا يا ذا القرنين إما أن تعذب وإما أن تتخذ فيهم حُسناً

لا يتفق ذلك مع العلم إطلاقا . هذه أول مرة أسمع أن الشمس تغيب في عين حمئة

17 – سورة الإسراء

44 – تسبحُ له السماوات السبع والأرض ومن فيهن وإن من شيء إلا يسبح بحمده ، ولكن لا تفقهون تسبيحهم إنه كان حليماً غفوراً

حسب علمي لا يوجد سبع سموات , إلا إذا كان العلم لم يكتشف ذلك بعد

16 – سورة النحل

58 – وإذا بُشر أحدهم بالأنثى ظل وجهه مُسوداً وهو كظيم

أليست في ذلك عنصرية ؟ إذ أنه يعطي الانطباع أن السواد نذير سوء

71 – والله فضل بعضكم على بعض في الرزق فما الذين فضلوا برادى رزقهم على ما ملكت أيمانهم فهم فيه سواء أفبنعمة الله يجحدون

لماذا يهب الله لبعض الناس أكثر من غيرهم . أين العدل ؟

93 – ولو شاء الله لجعلكم أمةً واحدةً ولكن يضل من يشاء ويهدي من يشاء ولتُسئلُن عما كنتم تعلمون

لماذا يفضل الله بعض الناس على غيرهم , ولماذا يحاسب الناس على أفعالهم إذا كان ذلك مقررا لهم سلفا . أليس ذلك غريبا ؟!.

106 – من كفر بالله بعد إيمانه إلا من أُكرة وقَلبُه مطمئن بالإيمان ، ولكن من شرح بالكفر صدراً فعليهم غضب من الله ولهم عذاب شديد

أليس ذلك نفاقاً . هل يريد الله منا أن نظهر غير ما نبطن ؟! .

قسطنطين بن أيوب | 38

15 – سورة الحجر

19 – والأرض مددناها وألقينا فيها رواسي وأنبتنا فيها من كل شيء موزون

مرة ثانية , الأرض مستديرة وليست منبسطة

14 – سورة إبراهيم

4 – وما أرسلنا رسول إلا بلسان قومه ليبين لهم فيضل الله من يشاء ويهدي من يشاء وهو العزيز الحكيم

إذا كان الله يهدي من يشاء ويضل من يشاء , فماذا سنفعل نحن البشر ولماذا نلام على أخطائنا

13 – سورة الرعد

2 – ألله الذي رفع السماوات بغير عمد ترونها ثم استوى على العرش وسخر الشمس والقمر كل يجرى لأجل مسمى يدبر الأمر يفصل الآيات ، لعلكم بلقاء ربكم توقنون

العلم يقرر أن الشمس ثابتة , إلا إذا كان ما يقصده النص القرآني أن الحركة هي الحركة المتكاملة لكوكبنا مع المجرة (المجرة اللبنية) [هذا الذي لم أفهمه شخصيا] . فإذا كان ذلك هو المقصود , فإن القول أن كلاً منهما يتحرك لفترة محدودة , فإنه قول خاطئ لأن ذلك يحدد حركة الشمس والقمر بالنسبة للأرض , وبطريقة أخرى, يجب أن يقال أن الشمس والقمر والكرة الأرضية يتحركون بالنسبة لبعضهم في الفضاء , وفوق ذلك فإذا ما أدخل موضوع الفضاء وموضوع حركتهم ضمن الفضاء في المعادلة فيجب أن يقال أن يتم ذلك مطلق وليس لفترة محدودة . وذلك لأن حركتهم المشتركة تجري بتسارع وتختلف باستمرار ؟! (أي أن ما جاء في القرآن يتنافى مع العلم)

42– وقد مكر الذين من قبلهم فلله المكر جميعاً يعلم ما تكسب كل نفس وسيعلم الكفار لمن عقبى الدار

حاشى لله أن يكون أمكر الماكرين , المكر صفة مكروهة لأي كان , فكيف بالله العظيم

12 - سورة يوسف

2 – إنا أنزلناه قرآناً عربياً لعلكم تعقلون

لماذا يكون القرآن باللغة العربية فقط . أنا مثلا لم يكن باستطاعتي فهم القرآن بالمعنى الصحيح لو لم أتعلم اللغة العربية . هل هي اللغة الوحيدة التي يتكلم بها الله في السماء .

11 – سورة هود

7 – وهو الذي خلق السماوات والأرض في ستة أيام وكان عرشه على الماء ليبلوكم أيكم أحسن عملاً ولئن قلت أنكم مبعوثون من بعد الموت ليقولن الذين كفروا إن هذا إلا سحر مبين

وهنا نحن نرى أن عرش الله مبنى فوق الماء

10 – سورة يونس

3 – إن ربكم الله الذي خلق السماوات والأرض في ستة أيام ثم استوى على العرش يدبر الأمر ، ما من شفيع إلا من بعد إذنه ، ذلكم الله ربكم فاعبدوه ، أفلا تذكرون

هذه أول مرة أسمع أن الله له عرش

21 – وإذا أذقنا الناس رحمة من بعد ضراء مستهم إذا لهم مكر في آياتنا قل الله أسرع مكراً ، إن رسلنا يكتبون ما تمكرون

طالما تعلمنا أن المكر من صفات الشيطان لا من صفات الله

111 – إن الله اشترى من المؤمنين أنفسهم وأموالهم بأن لهم الجنة يقاتلون في سبيل الله فيقتلون ويُقتلون وعداً عليه حقاً في التوراة والإنجيل والقرآن ومن أوفى بعهده من الله فاستبشروا ببيعكم الذي بايعتم به وذلك هو الفوز العظيم

أي أن الله يطلب من الناس أن يضحوا بكل شيء ليموتوا من أجله . هل خلقنا الله نقاتل ونَقتُل ونُقتَل من أجله , لماذا خلقنا إذاً

---

113 – ما كان للنبي والذين آمنوا أن يستغفروا للمشركين ولو كانوا أولي قربى من بعد ما تبين لهم أنهم أصحاب الجحيم

هذا تحريض للمؤمنين حتى ضد أفراد أسرهم . كيف للمرء أن يعادي أفراد أسرته مهما كان السبب

---

123 – يا أيها الذين آمنوا قاتلوا الذين يلونكم من الكفار وليجدوا فيكم غلظة واعلموا أن الله مع المتقين

عودة إلى غياب العطف في كتاب يفترض أن يحث على السلام والتسامح . ومن المحير أن يطلب من المؤمنين أن يقوموا بهذا العدوان من أجله في حين أنه يستطيع أن يرسل ملائكته لتنفيذ هذه الطلبات .ألا يدعوا ذلك إلى الغرابة .

23 – ياأيها الذين أمنوا لا تتخذوا آباءكم وإخوانكم أولياء إن استحبوا الكفر على الإيمان ومن يتولهم منكم فأولئك هم الظالمون

إنه لمن المستغرب أن يقوم الله بتحريض أفراد العائلة تجاه بعضهم . فليؤمن أبي وأخي وكل العائلة بما يريدون وأؤمن أنا بما أريد. وسيقوم الله بمحاسبة الناس في الآخرة . إذا اختاروا أهلي السبيل إلى جهنم فهذا شغلهم . فما الخطأ أن يكونوا أوليائي

28 – ياأيها الذين آمنوا إنما المشركون نجس فلا يقربوا المسجد الحرام بعد عامهم هذا وإن خفتم عيلة فسوف يغنيكم الله من فضله إن شاء ، إن الله عليم حكيم

لماذا اعتبار غير المؤمنين نجسين , غير طاهرين

29 – قاتلوا الذين لا يؤمنون بالله ولا باليوم الآخر ولا يحرمون ما حرم الله ورسوله ولا يدينون دين الحق من الذين أوتوا الكتاب حتى يعطوا الجزية عن يد وهم صاغرون

لماذا ينظر إلى غير المؤمنين باحتقار

73 - يا أيها النبي جاهد الكفار والمنافقين واغلظ عليهم ومأواهم جهنم وبئس المصير

لماذا كل هذه الكراهية تجاه غير المؤمنين . أين الإنسانية ؟ أين التعاطف

9 – سورة التوبة

5 – فإذا انسلخ الأشهر الحرم فاقتلوا المشركين حيث وجدتموهم وخذوهم واحصروهم واقعدوا لهم كل مرصد فإن تابوا وأقاموا الصلاة وآتوا الزكاة فخلوا سبيلهم ، إن الله غفور رحيم

لماذا هذا العداء لغير المؤمنين فليؤمن كل إنسان بما يشاء .

12 – وإن نكثوا أيمانهم من بعد عهدهم وطعنوا فى دينكم فقاتلوا أئمة الكفر ، إنهم لا إيمان لهم لعلهم ينتهون

ها نحن أمام العنف مرة ثانية

13 – ألا تقاتلون قوما نكثوا أيمانهم وهموا بإخراج الرسول وهم بدءوكم أول مرة أتخشونهم فالله أحق أن تخشوه إن كنتم مؤمنين

الدعوة للإنتقام بدل المصالحة

14 – قاتلوهم يعذبهم الله بأيديكم ويخزهم وينصركم عليهم ويشف صدورَ قوم موءمنين

أمر غريب أن يقول الله في القرآن "الكريم" الحث على القتال يخرج الكراهية من صدور المؤمنين

66 – ألئن خفف الله عنكم وعلم أن فيكم ضعفاً فإن يكن منكم مائة صابره يغلبوا مائتين وإن يكن منكم ألف يغلبوا ألفين بإذن الله والله مع الصابرين

وكأن النبي قد لاحظ أنه في الآية السابقة قد بالغ في مطالبه . إذا كان النص القرآني كلام الله فلماذا تبدأ الآية 66 " ألئن خفف الله عنكم " بدلاً من " ألئن خففت عنكم " , وإلا فمن هو صاحب النص .

67 – ما كان لنبى أن يكون له أسرى حتى يثخن فى الأرض ، تريدون عرض الدنيا والله يريد الأخرة والله عزيز حكيم

أليس القتل أسوأ من الأسر .

68 – لولا كتاب من الله سبق لمسكم فيما أخذتم عذاب عظيم

إنني أرى عكس ذلك . الناس يجب أن تعاقب إذا فعلوا أخطاء بعد استنارتهم .

69 – فكلوا مما غنمتم حلالاً طيباً واتقوا الله إن الله غفور رحيم

كيف يمكن لإنسان سوي أن يستمتع بمال مسلوب .

39 – وقاتلوهم حتى لا تكون فتنة ويكون الدين كله لله فإن انتهوا فإن الله بما يعملون بصير

لماذا يتم اللجوء دائما إلى القتال بدل اللجوء إلى وسائل مقبولة .

41 – واعلموا أنما غنمتم من شيء فإن لله خمسه وللرسول ولذي القربى واليتامى والمساكين وابن السبيل إن كنتم آمنتم بالله وما أنزلنا على عبدنا يوم الفرقان يوم التقى الجمعان والله على كل شيء قدير

مما يؤسف له أن الله ورسوله يطالبان بجزء من الغنائم .

60 – وأعدوا لهم ما استطعتم من قوة ومن رباط الخيل ترهبون به عدو الله وعدوكم وآخرين من دونهم لا تعلمونهم الله يعلمهم وما تنفقوا من شيء فى سبيل الله يوف إليكم وأنتم لا تُظلمون

هذه دعوة صريحة من الله القدير إلى الحرب والعنف بإسمه

65 – يأيها النبي حرض المؤمنين على القتال ، إن يكن منكم عشرون صابرون يغلبوا مائتين وإن يكن منكم مائة يغلبوا ألفاً من الذين كفروا بأنهم قوم لا يفقهون

كم هو أسلوب مرعب لحث الناس على الجهاد , الحرب المقدسة

8 – سورة الأنفال

12 – إذ يوحي ربك إلى الملائكة أني معكم فثبتوا الذين آمنوا سألقي في قلوب الذين كفروا الرعب فاضربوا فوق الأعناق واضربوا منهم كل بنان

لماذا يذكر الرعب والإرهاب في رسالة سماوية .

13 – ذلك بأنهم شاقوا الله ورسوله ومن يشاقق الله ورسوله فإن له شديد ألعقاب

لماذا يلجأ الله ورسوله إلى هذه القسوة .

15 – يأيها الذين آمنوا إذا لقيتم الذين كفروا زحفاً فلا تولوهم الأدبار

لماذا تتوقع الضرر من الآخرين دائماً . هذا يعكس ما في قلبك .

16 – ومن يولهم يومئذ دبره إلا متحرفاً لقتال أو متحيزاً إلى فئة فقد باء بغضب من الله ومأواه جهنم وبئس المصير

أين هي الرحمة التي ينتظرها الجميع من السماء .

30 – وإذ يمكر بك الذين كفروا ليثبتوك أو يقتلوك أو يخرجوك ويمكرون ويمكر الله والله خير الماكرين

أعتبر هذا النعت مهين لله

179 – ولقد ذرأنا لجهنم كثيراً من الجن والإنس لهم قلوب لا يفقهون بها ولهم أعين لا يبصرون بها ولهم آذان لايسمعون بها أولئك كالأنعام بل هم أضل أولئك هم الغافلون

مرة أخرى , لماذا ينعت الذين لا يقبلون تعاليم الإسلام بالأنعام الضالين

183 – وأملى لهم أن كيدي متين

لقد كنت أعتقد دائماً أن الله مسامح رحيم .

7 - سورة الأعراف

99 - أفأمنوا مكر الله فلا يأمن مكر الله إلا القوم الخاسرون

لم أكن أظن أن الله ماكر .

166 - فلما عتوا عن ما نهوا عنه قلنا لهم كونوا قردة خاسئين

لم أكن أظن أن الله يعاقب بهذه الطريقة .

172 - وإذ أخذ ربك من بني أدم من ظهورهم ذريتهم وأشهدهم على أنفسهم ألست بربكم قالوا بلى شهدنا أن تقولوا يوم القيامة إنا كنا عن هذا غافلين

مع أن بعض الناس يعتقدون أن الأطفال ينحدرون من ظهور آبائهم , ولكن ذلك يضحده العلم .

176 - ولو شئنا لرفعناه بها ولكنه أخلد إلى الأرض واتبع هواه فمثله كمثل الكلب إن تحمل عليه يلهث أو تتركه يلهث ذلك مثل القوم الذين كذّبوا بآياتنا فاقصص القصص لعلهم يتفكرون

من العار أن تصف الناس الذين لا يريدون الإسلام ديناً أن يوصفوا بالكلاب التي تلهث

51 – يا أيها الذين آمنوا لا تتخذوا اليهود والنصارى أولياء بعضهم أولياء بعض ومن يتولهم منكم فإنه منهم ، إن الله لا يهدى القوم الظالمين

ما هذه الكراهية لليهود المسيحيين وكيف أشعر بالكره تجاه والدي اليهودي أو أمي المسيحية وهما يحباني كل هذا الحب .

60 - قل هل أُنبئُكم بشر من ذلك مثوبةً عند الله من لَعَنَهُ اللهُ وغضبَ عليه وجعلَ منهُم القرَدةَ والخنازيرَ وعَبَدَ الطاغوتَ أولائكَ شرُ مكاناً وأضلُ عن سواء السبيل

لماذا يوصف اليهود بالقردة والمسيحيون بالخنازير

101 – يا أيها الذين آمنوا لا تسألوا عن أشياء إن تبد لكم تسؤكم وإن تسألوا عنها حين ينزل القرآن تبد لكم عفا الله عنها والله غفور حليم

أعتقد أنه أمر أساسي أن يسأل الإنسان عن أي شيء حتى يصل إلى الحقيقة المطلقة . فلماذا لا يريدنا القرآن أن نسأل عن أمور نجهلها أو أن يكون علمها مزعج لنا .

5 – سورة المائدة ،

6 – يأيها الذين أمنوا إذا قمتم إلى الصلاة فاغسلوا وجوهكم وأيديكم الى المرافق وامسحوا برءوسكم وأرجلكم إلى الكعبين وإن كنتم جُنُباً فاطهروا وإن كنتم مرضى أو على سفر أو جاء أحدكم من الغائط أو لامستم النساء فلم تجدوا ماءً فتيمموا صعيداً طيباً فامسحوا بوجوهكم وأيديكم منه ما يريد الله ليجعل عليكم من حرج ولكن يريد ليطهركم وليتم نعمته عليكم لعلكم تشكرون

مرة أخرى لماذا يساوي بين النساء والغائط وكيف يمكن أن ينظف المرء نفسه بالتراب .

33 – إنما جزاء الذين يحاربون الله ورسوله ويسعون في الأرض فساداً أن يقتلوا أو يصلبوا أو تقطع ايديهم وأرجلهم من خلاف أو ينفوا من الأرض ، ذلك لهم خزي في الدنيا ولهم فى الآخرة عذاب عظيم

إن في ذلك عنفاً غير مسبوق

37 – والسارق والسارقة فاقطعوا أيديهما جزاء بما كسبا نكالاً من الله والله عزيز حكيم

تصور أن تقطع يد إنسان لأنه اضطر لسرقة قطعة خبز لإطعام إبنه . هل يمكن لله أن يكون بهذه القسوة ؟ بالتأكيد يجب أن يكون في هذا العالم قليل من التعاطف كما أنه يكون من الأفضل إيجاد طريقة أخرى لمعاقبة اللصوص , مثال على ذلك أن توضع أيديهم في الأصفاد لفترة معينة لاشعارهم بالخجل .

91 – ستجدون آخرين يريدون أن يأمنوكم ويأمنوا قومهم كلما ردوا إلى الفتنة أركسوا فيها ، فإن لم يعتزلوكم ويلقوا إليكم السلم ويكفوا أيديهم فخذوهم واقتلوهم حيث ثقفتموهم وأولائكم جعلنا لكم عليهم سلطاناً مبيناً

ألا توجد وسيلة ألطف للتعامل مع الآخرين , فالمفروض أن الله ضد العنف بالمطلق .

144 – يا أيها الذين آمنوا لا تتخذوا الكافرين أولياء من دون المؤمنين ، أتريدون أن تجعلوا لله عليكم سلطاناً مبيناً

مثال آخر عن الكراهية تجاه الآخرين .

176 - "فللذكر مثل حظ الأنثيين "

أين العدل , يبدو أن الله يميز الذكور على الإناث .

77 – ألم تر إلى الذين قيل لهم كفوا أيديكم وأقيموا الصلاة وآتوا الزكاة فلما كتب عليهم القتال إذا فريق منهم يخشون الناس كخشية الله أو أشد خشية وقالوا ربنا لم كتبت علينا القتال لولا أخرتنا إلى أجل قريب قل متاع الدنيا قليل والآخرة خير لمن اتقى ولا تظلمون فتيلاً

آية أخرى تدعو للقتال .

82 - أفلا يتدبرون القرآن ولو كان من عند غير الله لوجدوا فيه اختلافاً كثيراً

ألى يدعو إلى الاستغراب أن كثيراً من الآيات تدعو إلى السلام والتسامح والعمل الطيب وهناك آيات تدعو إلى القتال والعنف والإرهاب .

84 – فقاتل في سبيل الله ، لا تكلف إلا نفسك وحرض المؤمنين عسى الله أن يكف بأس الذين كفروا والله أشد بأساً وأشد تنكيلاً

بينما يسأل الله الناس أن يحاربوا من أجله يطلب من رسوله أن يعتني فقط بنفسه

89 – ودوا لو تكفرون كما كفروا فتكونون سواء فلا تتخذوا منهم أولياء حتى يهاجروا في سبيل الله فإن تولوا فخذوهم واقتلوهم حيث وجدتموهم ولا تتخذوا منهم ولياً ولا نصيراً

عدم الثقة بأحد إلا بأتباعك , وكذلك يوجد عنف تجاه الآخرين

43 – يأيها الذين أمنوا لا تقربوا الصلاة وأنتم سكارى حتى تعلموا ما تقولون ولا جنباً إلا عابرى سبيل حتى تغتسلوا وإن كنتم مرضى أو على سفر أو جاء أحد منكم من الغائط أو لامستم النساء فلم تجدوا ماءً فتيمموا صعيداً طيباً فامسحوا بوجوهكم وأيديكم ، إن الله كان عفواً غفوراً

انني لا أتصور أن زوجتي أو قريباتي من النساء أو والدتي تساوي الغائط , كما أنني لا أقبل أن أنظف نفسي باستعمال التراب وما به من أوساخ .

74 – فليقاتل في سبيل الله الذين يشرون الحياة الدنيا بالآخرة ومن يقاتل فى سبيل الله فيقتل أو يغلب فسوف نؤتيه أجراً عظيماً

لماذا يكافأ الناس عندما يَقتلون أو يُقتلون ؟

75 – وما لكم لا تقاتلون في سبيل الله والمستضعفين من الرجال والنساء والولدان الذين يقولون ربنا أخرجنا من هذه القرية الظالم أهلها واجعل لنا من لدنك ولياً واجعل لنا من لدنك نصيراً

ها هو الله يدعوا الناس إلى القتال ثانيةً , ألا توجد وسيلة أخرى لمحاربة الطغيان . وكيف يكون أن الناس العاديين يحاولون التعايش السلمي المشترك بينما يدعو الله السعي إلى الحرب والمفروض أن يكون الأكثر رفقا ومحبة .

76 – الذين آمنوا يقاتلون في سبيل الله والذين كفروا يقاتلون فى سبيل الطاغوت ، فقاتلوا أولياء الشيطان ، إن كيد الشيطان كان ضعيفاً

مرة أخرى نحن مدعوون للقتال

25 – ومن لم يستطع منكم طولاً أن ينكح المحصنات المؤمنات فمن ما ملكت أيمانكم من فتياتكم المؤمنات والله أعلم بإيمانكم بعضكم من بعض ، فانكحوهن بإذن أهلهن وآتوهن أجورهن بالمعروف محصنات غير مسافحات, ولا متخذات أخدان ، فإذا أحصن فإن أتين بفاحشة فعليهن نصف ما على المحصنات من العذاب ذلك لمن خشى العنت منكم وأن تصبروا خير لكم والله غفور رحيم

هذه الآية تؤكد ما جاء في الآية 24 أي الجنس مقابل المال .

34 – الرجال قوامون على النساء بما فضل الله بعضهم على بعض وبما أنفقوا من أموالهم فالصالحات قانتات حافظات للغيب بما حفظ الله واللاتي تخافون نشوزهن فعظوهن واهجروهن في المضاجع واضربوهن فإن أطعنكم فلا تبغوا عليهن سبيلا ، إن الله كان علياً كبيراً

لا أحب أن أرى والدي يضرب والدتي . أنا لن اقوم بضرب زوجتي لأي سبب . وكذلك لماذا يفضل الله البعض عن البعض الآخر , خاصة إذا كانوا يقدمون له مالاً .
أما النساء الخيرات اللاتي يقدرن ما أعطى الله في غيابهن فإنهن "ساذجات"
إن هذه الآية هي من أسوأ ما قرأت في القرآن , فأنا لا أصدق أن هنالك نساء يقبلن هذا التحقير لهن من"ربهن"

4 – سورة النساء

3 – وإن خفتم ألا تقسطوا في اليتامى فانكحوا ما طاب لكم من النساء مثنى وثلاث ورباع فإن خفتم ألا تعدلوا فواحدة أو ما ملكت أيمانكم ، ذلك أدنى ألا تعدلوا

لماذا يسمح للرجال بتعدد الزوجات والسبايا .أن في ذلك تحقير للنساء

15 - ,واللاتي يأتين الفاحشة من نسائكم فاستشهدوا عليهن اربعة منكم فإن شهدوا فأمسكوهن في البيوت حتى يتوفاهن الموت أو يجعل الله لهن سبيلا

الآية 3 أعلاه تبيح للرجال فعل أي شيء تقريبا في حين تعاقب المرأة على أي شيء تفعل

24 – والمحصنات من النساء إلا ما ملكت أيمانكم كتاب الله عليكم وأحل لكم ما وراء ذلكم أن تبتغوا بأموالكم محصنين غير مسافحين فما استمتعتم به منهن فأتوهن أجورهن فريضة ولا جناح عليكم فيما تراضيتم به من بعد الفريضة ، إن الله كان عليماً حكيماً

ما الفرق بين هذا والدفع مقابل الجنس

151 – سنلقى فى قلوب الذين كفروا الرعب بما أشركوا بالله ما لم ينزل به سلطانا ومأواهم النار وبئس مثوى الظالمين

لا أعتقد أن الله يلقي الرعب في قلب أي كان

167 – وليعلم الذين نافقوا وقيل لهم تعالوا قاتلوا فى سبيل ألله أو إدفعوا قالوا لو نعلم قتالاً لاتبعناكم هم للكفر يومئذ أقرب منهم للإيمان ، يقولون بأفواههم ما ليس فى قلوبهم ، وألله أعلم بما يكتمون

لماذا يريد الله أن يحارب الناس من أجله فهو قادر على إرسال جيش من الملائكة ليحاربوا من أجله

195 – فاستجاب لهم ربهم أني لا أضيع عمل عامل منكم من ذكر أو أنثى بعضكم من بعض ،فالذين هاجروا وأخرجوا من ديارهم وأوذوا فى سبيلى وقاتلوا وقتلوا لأكفرن عنهم سيئاتهم ولأدخلنهم جنات تجرى من تحتها الأنهار ثوابا من عند الله والله عنده حسن الثواب

لماذا يحارب المرء ويموت من أجل الحصول على مكافأة دنيوية

3 – سورة آل عمران

6 – هو الذي يصوركم في الأرحام كيف يشاء لا إله إلا هو العزيز الحكيم

لا أرى لذلك معنى هذه الأيام حيث امكانية الاستنساخ والتدخل الطبي

---

28 – لا يتخذ المؤمنون الكافرين أولياء من دون المؤمنين ومن يفعل ذلك فليس من الله في شيء إلا أن تتقوا منهم تقاة ويحذركم الله نفسه وإلى الله المصير

لماذا لا يرضي المؤمنون عن رئاسة غير المؤمنين , فكثيراً ما يكون غير المؤمنين أفضل من المؤمنين . الله يطلب من المؤمنين أن يكونوا منافقين تجاه الآخرين

---

54 - ومكروا ومكر الله والله خير الماكرين

مستحيل أن يكون المكر من صفات الله

---

106 – يوم تبيض وجوه وتسود وجوه فأما الذين اسودت وجوههم أكفرتم بعد إيمانكم فذوقوا العذاب بما كنتم تكفرون

يبدو أن هناك تفرقة عنصرية من الذات الإلهية تجاه السود

---

107 - ,وأما الذين ابيضت وجوههم ففى رحمة ألله هم فيها خالدون

الظاهر أن الله يفضل الجنس الأبيض على الجنس الأسود . هذا وحي إلهي في قمة العنصرية ولا يصدق إطلاقاً . ماذا عن الملونين الذين لا هم من الجنس الأبيض ولا الأسود

193 - وقاتلوهم حتى لا تكون فتنة ويكون الدين لله فإن انتهوا فلا عدوان إلا على الظالمين

ألله ينشر الرسالة بالعنف .

216- كتب عليكم القتال وهو كره لكم وعسى أن تكرهوا شيئاً وهو خير لكم وعسى أن تحبوا شيئاً وهو شر لكم والله يعلم وأنتم لا تعلمون

لماذا يكتب القتال على أي كان

223 – نساؤكم حرث لكم فأتوا حرثكم أنى شئتم وقدموا لأنفسكم ,واتقوا الله واعلموا أنكم ملاقوه وبشر المؤمنين

لماذا تعتبر النساء حرثاً يؤتى في أي وقت

225 – لا يؤاخذكم الله باللغو في أيمانكم ولكن يؤاخذكم بما كسبت قلوبكم والله غفور رحيم

أي أن الله يطلب من المؤمنين أن يكذبوا وينافقوا

230- فإن طلقها فلا تحل له من بعد حتى تنكح زوجا غيره ، فإن طلقها فلا جناح عليهما أن يتراجعا إن ظنا أن يقيما حدود الله وتلك حدود الله يبينها لقوم يعلمون

أرى أن في ذلك عقاب للطرفين

2 – سورة البقرة

22 – الذي جعل لكم الأرض فراشاً والسماء بناءً وأنزل من السماء ماءً فأخرج به من الثمرات رزقاً لكم فلا تجعلوا لله أنداداً وأنتم تعلمون

الأرض مستديرة وليست منبسطة

29 – هو الذي خلق لكم ما في الأرض جميعاً ثم إستوى إلى ألسماء فسواهن سبع سماوات وهو بكل شيء عليم

حسب علمي لا يوجد سبع سماوات

65 – ولقد علمتم الذين اعتدوا منكم في السبت فقلنا لهم كونوا قردة خاسئين

لماذا يقوم الله بتحويل الإنسان إلى قرد

106 – ما ننسخ من آية أو ننسها نأت بخير منها أو مثلها ألم تعلم أن الله على كل شيء قدير

لماذا لا يكون الوحي الإلهي بدون خطأ بتاتاً من البدء ومن الممكن تغييره او تحسينه لاحقاً. هذا يعني أن الله أيضاً يخطىء

161 – إن الذين كفروا وماتوا وهم كفار أولئك عليهم لعنة الله والملائكه والناس اجمعين

لماذا يقوم الله والملائكة وكل الناس بلعنة أي إنسان

ولكن صدمتي الكبرى جائت عندما قرأت سورة الأحزاب رقم 33 آية 37 والتي تذكر أن الله سمح لنبيه محمد أن يعقد قرانه على إمراة إبنه بالتبني . ففي هذه الآية وبكل وضوح تذكر كلمة "زوجناكها" فبحثت عن هذه الكلمة في المعجم العربي وإذ بها تعني " زواج الرجل والمرأة ." عندها فكرت في نفسي إذا كلمة زواج موجودة في اللغة العربية الفصحى وتعني قران الرجل بالمرأة لماذا أصر الفرآن على ذكر كلمة نكاح البذيئة في القرآن كله بدل كلمة زواج . زيادة على ذلك إذا كلمة "نكاح" تعني زواج إذا لماذا لم يقول الله لنبيه محمد في سورة الأحزاب 33 آية 37 "نكحناكها" بدلا من "زوجناكها " . هذا كله في قمة الغرابة .

لقد وضعت في بعض الأحيان كلمات بين قوسين وذلك لتعريف كلمة أو عبارة أو جملة سابقة , وكان ذلك لتسهل للقارئ فهم الآية المعنية في القرآن . هنالك بعض الكلمات أو العبارات في القرآن الكريم من الصعب جداً ترجمتها لكي تعطي القارىء المعنى الصحيح , وللمثال :

1 ـ كلمة "سوبيريور" التي كتبتها مرارا في النص لتعني "أولياء" للتعبير عن من يتحكم أو من يقود الناس
2 ـ عبارة " وط يور رايت هاند اونز " أي "ما ملكت أيمانكم" التي ظهرت كثيرا في القرآن والتي تعني ما يمتلكه الرجال من النساء بالغنائم أو بشرائهم كسلعة من أسواق العبيد , واعدادهم تكون واحدة أو ألاف , وهم بالطبع موضع جاه للمالك بين القوم , والكلمة الوحيدة التي كان بقدرتي استعمالها في اللغة الإنجليزية لشرح هذا الوضع كانت كلمة"كابتفز"
3 ـ خلال كامل النص استعملت كلمة " بلنضرنج" باللغة الإنجليزية لتعني "غنائم" لشرح ما يؤخذ كسلب ونهب بعد الإنتصار في حالة الغزو والهجوم والحرب . وفي هذه الحالات كانت تؤخذ الأراضي والممتلكات ويقتل الرجال وتؤخذ النساء كسبايا والأطفال يباعون بدل اسلحة أو يؤخذون كعبيد
4 ـ كلمة "نكاح" تظهر في أماكن وسور عديدة في الفرآن . عندما بحثت عن معنى هذه الكلمة في المعجم العربي لاحظت أنها كانت ولا زالت تعني "الجماع الجنسي" .فسألت صديقي وعدد من المصلين الذين اجتمعت معهم في المسجد بما فيهم إمام المسجد عن ذكر هذه الكلمة وبهذه الكثرة في الفرآن جميعهم قالوا لي أن كلمة نكاح في القرآن تعني زواج . والظاهر أن عقد زواج في الإسلام هو " عقد نكاح"

كما يمكننا أن نرى صعوبة الترجمة . أما أنا فرأيي أن القرآن هو الأشد صعوبة في الترجمة , فقد كان علي أن أمضي وقتا طويلا في محاولة ترجمة أو فهم آية واحدة .

ونتيجة لما تقدم وحيث أنني أعتبر أن لغتي العربية أصبحت جيدة فقد قررت أن أكتب هذا الكتاب باللغتين العربية والإنجليزية معا , فسيكون النص الإنجليزي على اليسار والنص العربي على اليمين . فقد تمت الكتابة سورة بعد سورة حسب ورودها في القرآن, وكذلك كل آية مع رقمها والصفحة التي وردت بها في القرآن . وكذلك لكي أسهل على القارئ المقارنة بين النصين العربي والإنجليزي . أما الآيات الواردة في اللغة العربية فهي منقولة حرفياً عن نسخة حفص من القرآن مكتوبة بالعربية الحديثة . كما أنها أكثر النسخ استعمالاً , وعليه فإن الكتابة باللغتين يقصد منه التسهيل على من يشكك بدقة الترجمة أن يرجع إلى النص العربي للتأكد من الحقائق . وهكذا يتأكدون أنني قد نقلت رسالة الآيات بأكثر دقة ممكنه ودون أي محاولة لسوء التفسير أو تشويه المعنى على القارئ الإنجليزي وقد كانت بعض الآيات طويلة ولن يكون لترجمتها إضافة لمحتويات هذا الكتاب .وفي مثل هذه الحالات فقد استشهدت فقط بالأجزاء التي لدي ملاحظة عليها وقد وضعتها بين هلالين وبذلك تكون ترجمتي لما هو بين الهلالين فقط.

وعليه ففي كل صفحة من الكتاب يجد القارئ السور التي لي اعتراض عليها مع ملاحظات حول سبب ذلك الموقف . يرجى ملاحظة أنه على طول الكتاب فقد استعملت الجمع بدل المفرد عند ذكرالله وذلك الجمع في اللغة العربية يستعمل للتعظيم .

فاتحه

بخصوص تنسيق هذا الكتاب

كان القصد من البداية أن أكتب هذا الكتاب باللغة الإنجليزية ولكنني خشيت أن يفترض القراء بحجة أن ترجمتي لبعض الآيات لا تنقل المعنى المقصود في القرآن . وكلنا نعلم أن الترجمة من لغة لأخرى ليست عملية سهلة فإن الترجمة الحرفية لا يمكن أن تكون ممكنة حيث أن كلمة واحدة في لغة ما تحتاج إلى جملة في لغة أخرى لأن تلك الكلمة غير موجودة في لغات ثانية . كما أن من الممكن أن الكلمة المرادفة لكلمة في لغات ثانية قد تعطي معنى مختلفاً إذا استعملت في سياق ما .
كما أنه في القرآن يوجد آيات في غاية الوضوح , بينما هنالك آيات صعبة الفهم حتى على من هم ضالعون باللغة العربية .بل أن هناك آيات اختلف في تفسيرها بعض اكثر المختصين في الدين الإسلامي حيث اعطوا تفسيرات مختلفة لمعناها , ولكي أعطي مثلاً .
"هل الشمس تغيب في نبع ماء ساخن , ام هي تغيب في طين ساخن , ام هي تغيب في ماء موحل " ذلك متروك لاي شخص أن يختار . وقد اخترت أنا ترجمتها " أن الشمس تغيب في نبع ماء ساخن " لان ذلك أكثر الأمور منطقية (وإن كنت لا أؤمن بذلك) .
هنالك عدة حالات مشابهة وقد قصدت أن أتجنب ذكرها لكي لا أقع في فخ سوء ترجمة المعنى المقصود في القرآن .

نيتي دراسة العهد القديم والعهد الجديد لأتمكن من إتخاذ القرار المناسب لحياتي. وقد قال والدي " نحن على ثقة أنك اتخذت القرار الصحيح فيما يختص بموضوع التحول. وسوف يكون علينا أن ننتظر لنرى أن كنت ستختار اليهودية أو المسيحية . وفي كلا الحالتين فإنها ستكون فكرة ممتازة لو قررت أن تكتب عن تجربتك لكي يستفيد منها آخرون ممن يفكرون بالتحول إلى الإسلام " . وبعد تفكير طويل قررت أن أفعل ذلك , وهو ما يلي :

الإنجليزية لا يمكن أن تنقل بدقة نصوص القرآن والحديث .
وأذ قلت لوالدي أنه يعلم أنني لا أقرأ اللغة العربية أجابني بأن هذه مهمتي وإذا بقيت على رغبتي بالتحول بعد هذه الدراسة فأننى سنحترم رغبتك وربما نتحول أنا ووالدتك معك فأننا نثق بذكائك وأنك لم تتخذ هذا الموقف إلا بعد دراسة مستفيضة , وربما يكون قد فاتنا طيلة حياتنا أشياء مهمة في الإسلام . إبتسمت , ووعدته بصدق أنني سأقوم بذلك فابتسم بدوره واقترب مني وصافحني وقبلني على وجنتي وغادر الغرفة
لقد احتجت إلى ثلاث سنوات لدراسة اللغة العربية قراءة واستيعاباً تاماً , وقد احتفظت هذه الفترة على علاقتي بصديقي المسلم كما واصلت قراءة القرآن باللغة الإنجليزية كلما سنحت الفرصة .
وقد جاء الوقت لكي أبدأ دراسة القرآن باللغة العربية وسوف أتبع ذلك بدراسة الحديث ,وكذلك بدأت أضع ملاحظاتي حول أمور لا أتفق معها أو أمور أراها بلا معنى.

علي أن أعترف إنه بعد قراءة النص العربي للقرآن, وجدت فرقاً بالمعنى بين النصين العربي والإنجليزي . وبالنهاية , فقد لاحظت أن هنالك عدة أمور غير قابلة للتطبيق في واقع الحياة لعدة أسباب مما أقنعني بأن الإسلام لا يناسبني , وقد أخبرت صديقي بقراري , فلم يظهر عليه امتعاض واستمرت علاقتنا الودية .
وفي نفس ذلك اليوم وخلال تناول العشاء مع والداي أخبرتهما أنه بعد دراسة القرآن قررت عدم اعتناق الإسلام , وقد لاحظت مدى سعادتهما لسماع ذلك , وبشكل خاص والدتي التي بكت فرحاً . وقد سألني والدي عن رأيي في "الحديث" فأخبرته أن ما قرأته في القرآن كان كافياً لاتخاذ قراري , فلم يكن هناك حاجة لدراسة الحديث .
أما في ما يختص بالمستقبل , فإنني لست واثقاً أن كنت سأنتمي إلى الدين اليهودي أو المسيحي حيث أن في

لمعرفة المزيد. وهكذا فقد قدم لي نسخة من القرآن الكريم باللغة الإنجليزية لمزيد من الاستنارة . وعندما عدت إلى البيت مساءً وجلست مع والداي على مائدة العشاء لمح والدي الكتاب في يدي , سألني عن محتوى ذلك الكتاب فأجبته أنه القرآن الكريم وأنني بصدد التحول إلى الإسلام , وفجأة أحسست أن الجو قد توتر وساد الصمت بدل الجو المرح الذي امتازت به جلساتنا , وبدا لي أن والداي قد أصابتهما حيرة فيما يقولان أو يفعلان . وقد انشغلنا في التهام طعامنا بسرعة لتلافي المزيد من الحديث . وبسبب هذا الجو المشحون الذي ظهرت اثاره على وجهي والداي فقد استأذنت منهما أن أذهب إلى غرفتي لأن علي الكثير من الواجبات الدراسية .

إستلقيت على سريري وأخذت أفكر في ما عساي قد فعلت , وما هي إلى قرابة الساعة حتى قرع والدي باب الغرفة وتوجه نحوي وبدا لي من احمرار عينيه وصوته أنه كان قد بكى , ثم جلس على طرف السرير وتوجه إلي قائلاً " يا بني أود أن أطلب منك جميلاً وأطلب منك أن تعدني بأنك ستقوم به " .وقلت لوالدي "أنني سأنفذ طلبك كما كنت أفعل دائماً ولكن لا تطلب مني أن أتراجع عن رغبتي باعتناق الإسلام " . فأجابني أنه بإمكاني أن أعتنق الإسلام برضى والداي ولكن بشرط أن تلبي الجميل الذي سأطلبه منك . فسألته عن الأمر الذي يطلبه مني فقال "أن تعدني بان لا يتم التحول إلا بعد دراسة الإسلام ومعرفة كل شيء عنه , فإن توصلت بعد الدراسة أنك ما زلت راغباً في اعتناقه , فإن ذلك من حقك وأنها حياتك ولك أن تتخذ أي قرار يرضيك". قلت لوالدي عندها أنه من أجل ذلك أحضرت القرآن , فقال لي أن ذلك لا يكفي , فإن الإسلام يقوم على دعامتين متلازمتين أحدهما القرآن وفيه تعاليم الأسلام وثانيهما ما يسمى "الحديث" وهو يعلن ويشرح أقوال وأفعال رسول الإسلام محمد . ويجب أن تتم دراسة الأمرين باللغة العربية لأن الترجمة

وأشاركها في تناول القربان . وهكذا فقد كنت في صراع بين الديانتين وإن كان يراودني ميل إلى الديانة المسيحية .
وعندما وصلت إلى المرحلة الجامعية التقيت بزميل من بلاد الهند وسرعان ما نشأت بيننا صداقة متينة . ولقد لفت نظري بقوة أنه يصلي عدة مرات يومياً لدرجة أنه لطالما أن كنا نتمشى معاً ثم يفاجئني بأنه قد حان الوقت له أن يؤدي الصلاة وعندها كان يخرج من جيبه منديلاً يفرده على الأرض في زاوية ثم يركع ويبدأ الصلاة . وإذ بدا لي غريباً أن يصلي المرء بهذه الكثرة سألته عن ذلك أخبرني أن ذلك مفروض في الدين الإسلامي . بطبيعة الحال لم يكن لذلك أي أثر على علاقتنا وكان علي أن أحترم خصوصيته إضافة إلى أنه كان انساناً طيباً وصديقاً جيداً وقد حصل مرة أن مررنا بقرب مسجد فاستأذن مني أن يدخل إلى المسجد ليصلي بينما أنتظره في الخارج . وفي احدى المرات تكرر ذلك ولكنه قال لي أنه بإمكاني الدخول معه إلى المسجد وأن أقف أو أجلس في الجزء الخلفي من المسجد وقد فعلت ذلك بتردد . وقد أدهشني كيف أنهم يقفون في صفوف مستقيمة ثم يقفون ويركعون سوياً بصمت بينما يردد (الإمام)- القائد- آيات من القرآن الكريم . لقد كان ذلك الجو شديد الورع والسكينة , وقد تكررت مرافقتي لصديقي بعدها , وكنت في كل مرة أخرج في حالة من السكينة والرضا والورع . وفي مرة سألني صديقي عن رأيي في ما رأيت واختبرت خلال زياراتي , فأجبته أنني في غاية التأثر . ومر عام علي وأنا أذهب إلى المسجد يوم الجمعة وإلى الكنيس يوم السبت وإلى الكنيسة يوم الأحد . وقد كان والداي على علم بصديقي المسلم وأنني رافقته عدة مرات إلى المسجد ولم يبديا أي اعتراض على ذلك .

وعندما سألني صديقي مرة أن كان خطر في بالي أن أتحول إلى الإسلام قلت له أنني فكرت بالأمر ولكنني ما زلت بحاجة

مقدمه

ولد كاتب هذه السطور في محيط يهودي-مسيحي حيث كان والدي يهودياً ملتزماً من روسيا بينما كانت والدتي مسيحية من بلغاريا . وكانا قد تزوجا زواجاً مدنياً حيث أن والدي رفض أن يتزوج زواجاً مسيحياً بينما رفضت والدتي أن تتزوج في الكنيس. ومع ذلك فقد بارك زواجهما كاهن مسيحي و حاخام يهودي , وقد كان الحب الذي جمع بين والداي ملحوظاً في كل ما يفعلانه , وكم كان يخطر في بالي انه لو كنت لي أن أتزوج أن تكون علاقتي الزوجيه نموذجية كحياتهما , وحيث أنه لم يكن لي أخوة أو أخوات فقد سألت والدتي عن السبب فقالت أن ذلك عائد لصعوبة في الحمل .
كان والدي يريد أن أكون يهودياً بينما كانت والدتي ترغب أن أكون مسيحياً وقد بذل كل منهما أن يستميلني لجهته . أما أنا فقد كنت أرافق والدي إلى الكنيس كما كنت أرافق والدتي إلى الكنيسة كلما كان ذلك ممكناً . وكثيراً ما كانت والدتي تقول لي أن المسيح قد حقق كل نبوءات العهد القديم وأنه هو المسيح الذي ما زال اليهود ينتظرونه عبثاً .
وقد أراد والدي عندما كنت صغيراً أن يجري لي عملية الختان كما هو في الدين اليهودي إلا أن ذلك كان يقابل بالرفض من قبل والدتي إلى أن تم الإتفاق بينهما أن يتم الختان ثم يتبعها العماد وعلى أن يترك لي حرية اختيار الدين الذي يناسبني عندما أكبر . كان هذا الإتفاق بينهما غريباً فعندما كنت أرافق والدي إلى الكنيس كنت أضع (ألقلنسوة) – غطاء رأس يستعمله اليهود- وكنت أحس بمدى سعادة والدي بذلك , كما كنت أشعر بسعادة والدتي عندما كنت أرافقها إلى الكنيسة

آيات قرآنية حالت دون تحول شخص من ثقافة مسيحية يهودية إلى الإسلام

قسطنطين بن أيوب

عندما علم صديق مسيحي أنني أريد التحول إلى الإسلام أنذرني أنه يجب علي أن أقطع في البدء القلفة من العضو الذكري وإذا لم يعجبني الإسلام لسبب ما وأردت أن أرتد فيجب علي أن أكون مستعداً لقطع رأسي . قلت له أنني الآن مختوناً وأنا واثق أنني لن أرتد

لحسن حظي فإن المعلومات الموجودة في هذا الكتاب أنقذت رأسي , وآمل أن تنقذ رؤوس الكثيرين .

www.ingramcontent.com/pod-product-compliance
Lightning Source LLC
Chambersburg PA
CBHW021425070526
44577CB00001B/57